SUB COMMANDER

Tactics and Strategy
for WWII Submarine Simulations

RICHARD G. SHEFFIELD

COMPUTE! Publications,Inc.**abc**

A Capital Cities/ABC, Inc. Company
Greensboro, North Carolina

Printed in the United States of America

10 9 8 7 6 5 4 3 2 1

ISBN 0-87455-127-7

The author and publisher have made every effort in the preparation of this book to insure the accuracy of the information. However, the information in this book is sold without warranty, either
express or implied. Neither the author nor COMPUTE! Publications, Inc. will be liable for any
damages caused or alleged to be caused directly, indirectly, incidentally, or consequentially by the
information in this book.

The opinions expressed in this book are solely those of the author and are not necessarily those of
COMPUTE! Publications, Inc.

COMPUTE! Publications, Inc., Post Office Box 5406, Greensboro, NC 27403, (919)
275-9809, is a Capital Cities / ABC, Inc. company, and is not associated with any
manufacturer of personal computers. *GATO* is a trademark of Spectrum Holobyte, Inc.
Silent Service is a trademark of MicroProse. *Sub Battle Simulator* is a trademark of
Epyx, Inc.

Contents

Preface

You've just been given command of a crisp and clean new fleet-class submarine. Your crew is well trained and made up of the best men available from other combat-proven boats. However, there is still one more item that needs attention— you, the commander. The responsibility for success or failure rides squarely on the shoulders of the "Old Man," the skipper. If the commander is not highly trained and experienced, the chances for a successful patrol are slim.

That's where this book comes in. This is the first book of any kind to thoroughly examine, explain, and illustrate the attack tactics used by sub commanders during the Second World War. You will need practice and seasoning to win. *Sub Commander: Tactics and Strategy for WWII Submarine Simulations* provides both.

The lessons include explanations and illustrations of basic attack philosophy, 15 different attack tactics, and defensive strategy and maneuvers. After mastering all this, you can go deep into the heart of enemy-controlled waters, stalk and sink thousands of tons of shipping, and live to brag about it.

Seasoning is also important. Many commands were lost during the first or second encounter with the enemy. With this book, you'll not only benefit from the experience of Richard Sheffield's hundreds of successful war patrols with all the popular simulations, but you'll also examine the Congressional-Medal-of-Honor-winning night attack of Commander Ramage and the USS *Parche*. You'll read the actual words of Commander Richard O'kane, of the USS *Tang*, as he describes how he set three tankers ablaze off of Formosa. You will learn how Commander J. W. Coe of the USS *Skipjack* and his crew pulled off the first recorded sinking with a "down-the-throat shot." And three other sinkings are also described in the captain's own words.

Finally, you'll benefit from the experience of many other

game players as you read the chapters which give tips and hints for playing:

Silent Service
GATO
Up Periscope!
Sub Battle Simulator

So flip your cap around backwards, peer through the periscope, and in the words of the U. S. Sub Force Commander, Vice Admiral C. A. Lockwood, "Sink 'em all!"

Acknowledgments

For their help and contributions to this book, I'd like to thank:

The excellent staff at the Still Picture Branch of the National Archives for helping me locate the photographs used herein and for making it so easy.

The professional staff and research assistants at the Naval Historical Center in Washington, D.C. for their invaluable assistance.

The Naval Institute Press for allowing me to use their account of the USS *Parche*'s historic engagement.

David L. Edwards W.G.S.C for his help and interest.

And of course, my wonderful wife Valarie for her continuing support.

CHAPTER 1

The USS *PARCHE*
vs.
All Hell

1
The USS *Parche* vs. All Hell

Great commanders make the difference between success and failure aboard a submarine. You, as the commander during a sub simulation, will make the decisions which either move you rapidly up in rank or sink your boat with all hands lost.

Aggressive rugged individualism describes most of the great sub commanders of the Second World War. These men generally operated alone and out of contact with superiors for extended periods of time. Their success depended on their ability to take their formal training and adapt it to the various situations they encountered and to improvise when called for.

These were not men who went strictly by the book. Commanders who tried this approach early in the war were not successful and were quickly replaced. Great commanders used the book as a guide and were quick to toss it out the window if they thought there was a better way of doing things.

To be a great sub commander you will have to use a similar approach. When attacking, devise an aggressive plan but don't fall in love with it. In submarine warfare, things can change very rapidly, and, as your situation changes, so must your plans. Be aggressive and adaptable, and your success as a sub commander will follow.

One of these aggressive and adaptable sub commanders was Commander Lawson P. (Red) Ramage. Ramage and his boat, the USS *Parche*, had been assigned to patrol a heavily traveled area off of Formosa which had come to be known as Convoy College. A patrol into the Convoy College area was sure to earn you a master's in convoy attack methods. In a brilliant night-surface attack off the coast of Formosa, Red

Ramage displayed all of the traits of the great sub commanders: He was brave, aggressive, adaptable, and showed excellent seamanship.

The following is an account of this attack as described in
United States Submarine Operations in World War II by Theodore
Roscoe (Copyright 1949, U.S. Naval Institute, Annapolis, Mary-
land, pages 343–346). This volume is an excellent source of
information regarding sub operations and is highly recommended.

Parche vs. All Hell (Commander Lawson P. Ramage)

Parche, Hammerhead, and *Steelhead* (Parks' Pirates) were
off Formosa on the morning of July 30, [1944] going about
their business like any well-organized submarine wolf-
pack. So far, business had been slow and pretty much
routine—that is, slow and routine so far as submarine
warfare is concerned.

Then, at 1030 in the morning of the 30th, *Steelhead*
(Commander D. L. Whelchel) sighted a convoy's smoke.
Steelhead trailed. The convoy was under an umbrella of air
protection, and Whelchel's submarine was unable to attack during the day. But at 2015 *Steelhead* got off a message to pack-mate *Parche*, giving the course and speed of
the Japanese ships. Ramage put *Parche* on the estimated
track and sent her plunging along the surface, top speed.

Midnight, and the two submarines were overhauling
the quarry. By 0300, morning of the 31st, *Steelhead* was
boring in on the attack. At 0332 Whelchel opened fire,
aiming six torpedoes at a tanker and a large freighter. One
torpedo was seen to hit the freighter, and a few moments
later a mushroom of black smoke surged up from the
tanker. Whelchel maneuvered to fire four stern shots at
another freighter. Two Japanese rockets soared in the
night, signaling the convoy's alarm.

These flares were seen by *Parche*. Ramage's submarine had made contact with one of the convoy's escorts
about 30 minutes earlier, and was driving forward with
crew at battle stations to strike the convoy's flank. Glare
of the rockets now revealed several large ships in silhou-
ette and three escorts rushing about. One of the escorts
was ahead of *Parche* and to the starboard. Two were on
the submarine's port, between *Parche* and the convoy. As

Sub involved in successful surface action.

5

one of these was bearing down on Ramage and company, Ramage decided the pattern needed some fast alteration.

Running the submarine at full speed, he started a circular swing to draw away from the oncoming escort. The A/S vessel continued on its course while *Parche* continued her circle which brought her in behind the stern of the second port-side escort.

"This reverse spinner play apparently confused the opposition," Ramage recalled afterward. "*Parche* was now between the escorts and their convoy, but while this maneuver was going on the entire [Japanese] convoy had reversed its field and was now heading directly for *Parche*."

Ramage picked out the closest target for the first shot—medium-sized freighter. But the range had been overestimated. Before the set-up could be made, the ship was only 450 yards away. Sharp full right rudder slid the submarine out of the freighter's path, and *Parche*'s bridge personnel could almost feel the breeze as the freighter went by at a scant 200 yards.

Ramage swung the submarine and opened fire with two bow shots. The alerted freighter managed a lucky zig, and the torpedoes missed. But the freighter's swing blocked the rush of an escort, and a moment later *Parche*'s lookouts spotted two tankers off to starboard. Starting a run for these targets, Ramage got in a stern shot at the freighter, and a thumping explosion registered a hit. A five-minute dash brought *Parche* within torpedo shot of the tankers.

Ramage fired four torpedoes at the leading tanker, then swung *Parche* hard right to fire three at the second tanker. The leading tanker collected the first salvo from cutwater to wake. The first torpedo blew the ship's bow to pieces. The next three ploughed into the tanker's midsection, quarter and stern. The ship went under immediately, leaving only a small patch of burning oil to mark the spot. The second tanker, struck near the bow by two torpedoes, staggered and slowed down, but kept on going. So did *Parche*, and she didn't slow down.

Every escort in the convoy and all of the remaining ships were now wheeling and milling. As though his submarine were a PT-boat, Ramage (whose *nom de guerre* was "Captain Red") drove into the center of the traffic jam, shooting everything. The convoy shot back everything. Ensued the maddest surface action yet fought by a submarine in the Pacific. Weaving and dodging through the convoy like a rodeo broncho attacking a herd of wild bulls, *Parche* struck at one *maru* after another. Ramage fired torpedo after torpedo as the enemy returned fusillades of glowing tracer and screaming shells. The scene blazed and roared with the din of an exploding fireworks factory. Hard right, hard left, the submarine swerved and veered. In her forward and after torpedo rooms the sweating men grunted, swore and labored like Vulcan's blacksmiths to load the tubes. Above, the T.D.C. operator "played the organ" at pinwheel pace, somehow keeping up with the spate of target data which came down from the bridge. On the bridge, at 0423, Ramage and companions were watching two A/S vessels close in—and Ramage was planning the next dodge—when a small, fast *maru* loomed up on the starboard bow, rushing to ram.

"We felt like a mouse at a bridge party," Ramage described the sensation. "I called the engine house to pour in all the oil they had."

Halfway across the rammer's bow, Ramage threw *Parche*'s rudder full right. Ship and submarine passed in the night with elbow room at less than 50 feet. This, as any navigator knows, is the width of a safety-razor blade. The shave left *Parche* boxed in by small craft on both sides and an oncoming passenger-cargo vessel looming up like the Flatiron Building dead ahead. Left with no alternative but a down-the-throat salvo, Ramage fired three bow shots at the advancing menace. The first torpedo missed. The next two were on the nose. The ship came to a rumbling stop as if she had run her bow into a mud bank. Ramage drove the submarine forward, then swung hard left to bring the stern tubes to bear. Firing a single, he saw the torpedo strike the vessel amidships. At 0442, as Ramage was maneuvering in for the final shot, the ship put its heavy head under the sea. Then, with a rush, it was gone.

Ramage glanced about for something else to shoot at, while the residue of the convoy, firing indiscriminately, looked for the submarine.

"There were still several small craft and escorts

around, but no worthwhile targets that we could see. I decided to put some distance between us and this hornet's nest."

As *Parche* hauled clear, distant explosions could be heard. *Steelhead* was attacking a remnant of the convoy which had run in that direction. At 0449 Whelchel fired four torpedoes at a large passenger-cargoman, and another salvo of four at a big freighter. The freighter was seen to sprout lifeboats and then go under. Whelchel was maneuvering to finish off the passenger-cargo carrier when an enemy plane attacked in the morning dusk and drove *Steelhead* deep.

Parche, in the meantime, was putting the "hornet's nest" astern. As she hauled away, one of the A/S vessels challenged her by searchlight, sending "AA-AA." This somewhat surprising flash was noted by a *Parche* signalman, Courtland Stanton, with the comment: "Those [Japanese] probably have a lot of forms to fill out, too."

Doubtless one of the forms filled out by the Japanese convoy's survivors reported the loss of some 39,000 tons of merchant shipping. As determined by post-war inquest of the joint Army-Navy Assessment Committee, *Steelhead* was responsible for the sinking of the 7,169-ton freighter *Dakar Maru* and the 8,195-ton transport *Fuso Maru*. Both submarines were credited with the destruction of the 8,990-ton transport *Yoshino Maru*. And *Parche* was credited with the sinking of *Koei Maru*, a 10,238-ton tanker, and *Manko Maru*, passenger-cargoman, 4,471 tons.

The Submarine Service credited Commander Lawson P. Ramage with something more. That credit is expressed in the following paragraphs—excerpts from the monograph with which the Submarine Force Board of Awards recommended Commander Ramage for the Congressional Medal of Honor:

"The personal daring and outstanding skill displayed by the Commanding Officer in his series of attacks against a large heavily escorted enemy convoy, consisting of tankers, transports, and freighters, conducted on 31 July, is one of the outstanding attacks in the submarine warfare to date, with action packed into every minute of this forty-six minute battle against the enemy. Attaining the ultimate in aggressiveness, exceptional courage, personal heroism, and bearing, the Commanding Officer sagaciously and with consummate skill, fired nineteen torpedoes in forty-six minutes to obtain fourteen or fifteen hits in this brilliant night surface attack.

"By a brilliant act of stratagem the Commanding Officer penetrated the strong escort screen; and, although hemmed in on all sides by ships and escorts trying to maneuver and deliver counter-attacks, he daringly closed to a favorable firing position from which to launch his torpedoes. With a well executed stern shot, he succeeded in damaging a freighter. Following up with a series of bow and stern shots, he sank the leading tanker and damaged a second tanker. Despite the grave problem of machine-gun fire and flares from escorts, near proximity of vessels, some as close as 200 yards, he successfully delivered two forward reloads to sink a transport. At the same time, he commenced maneuvering to avoid the nearest escort's gunfire and obtain a stern shot at a damaged tanker that had now manned her guns. As he reached a firing position, the first fusillade of the tanker's 4" or 5" shells passed close overhead and slightly forward. Because of the accuracy and intense firepower of additional enemy 20 mm. and 40 mm. increasing the possibilities of casualties, all lookouts and spare hands were sent below, with the exception of the Bridge Quartermaster who volunteered to remain on the TBT. The Commanding Officer, with utter disregard for personal safety, courageously remained at his station, on the bridge, despite the hail of bullets and shells, in order to maneuver his ship more effectively and score hits with his stern tubes. Simultaneously with his sinking the damaged tanker and while trying to close a large transport, he was forced to commence evasive maneuvers to avoid a fast transport or freighter bearing down, apparently intent on ramming him, and also in order to avoid concentrated machine-gun fire of the two nearby escorts. With bullets and shells flying all around, he ordered emergency full speed ahead and swung the stern of the *Parche* as she crossed the bow of the onrushing transport or freighter, clearing this enemy ship by less than fifty feet!

"Although now boxed in by escorts and the large

transport dead ahead, the Commanding Officer delivered three smashing down-the-throat bow shots and stopped the target. With high speed and expert seamanship, he tenaciously attacked again, scoring a killing hit with a reloaded stern torpedo.

"At break of dawn, with enemy escorts' counter-attacks becoming too accurate to justify further attack and risk, *Parche* cleared the area, thus having damaged one enemy ship and sunk four others in forty-six minutes. In another encounter, a 300 ton patrol vessel was sunk by gunfire.

"The counter-attacks by the enemy against *Parche* during her series of aggressive surface torpedo attacks upon the convoy on 31 July 1944 were probably the most intensive and thorough counter-attacks ever encountered by a submarine engaged in surface approaches and attacks against the enemy. Only exceptional seamanship, outstanding personal heroism and extreme bravery of *Parche*'s Commanding Officer saved this submarine from serious damage if not total destruction by enemy gunfire and ramming.

"The Commanding Officer's courage and fearless actions in remaining on the bridge of his submarine during intense and accurate enemy gunfire in order to maintain the offensive at all times, enabled him to control his ship skillfully and efficiently, launch his torpedoes effectively and evade the enemy's vigorous efforts to destroy *Parche*."

Between the lines of official rhetoric, one sees a young man with carrot-colored hair and clamped jaw, clinging to the bridge-frame of an embattled submarine and determined to fight it out against all opposition. Queried about the action later, Ramage made a brief reply to an interviewing journalist:

"I got mad."

Commander Lawson P. Ramage received the Congressional Medal of Honor.

CHAPTER 2

Pigboats, U-Boats, and Fleet Subs

2
Pigboats, U-Boats, and Fleet Subs

The German U-boats of World War I taught the whole world a lesson in the effectiveness and importance of submarine warfare. With this in mind, the U.S. government began serious submarine development during the 1920's and 1930's. The result of this effort was generally known as the S-boat.

S-boats were designed primarily for defensive purposes, had a relatively short range, and were slow in comparison to the other members of the fleet. These vessels were in the range of 850–1000 tons, had a top submerged speed of 10 knots, and a top surface speed of 14 knots. The interior of these ships was cramped at best and, due to the lack of air-conditioning, the atmosphere became quite pungent during extended dives or when operating in tropical waters. Due to this minor inconvenience it is not surprising that the S-boats acquired the nickname, pigboats.

With the Japanese threat in the Pacific becoming stronger, it became necessary to develop a submarine capable of operating with the fleet as part of a task force if needed. Following this doctrine, the boat commonly known as the fleet sub was developed. This fleet sub had to be able to travel the extended distances of the Pacific and keep up with fast aircraft carriers and destroyers. As it turned out however, the name fleet sub was a misnomer as they never did operate in this manner during the war.

All of the fleet-type subs were not exactly alike, but the operational features were generally similar. They could stay at sea for 75–80 days at a time and cover 10,000 or more miles without having to refuel. Maximum operational speeds were

10 knots submerged and 20 knots on the surface. These vessels were state-of-the-art in terms of seaworthiness, habitability, and survivability. The interiors, while small, were much more comfortable than subs of other navies. The food was the best in the navy, and movies were shown during slow periods in the forward torpedo room. All-welded, double-hull construction allowed the subs to hide in the comparative safety of extremely deep water. Depths in excess of 600 feet were recorded by some subs during the war.

A Walk Through a Fleet Sub

A tour of a fleet-type sub might start by entering the sub through a hatch (one of six) in the bow of the ship which would lead into the forward torpedo room. This is the first of eight watertight compartments. This room is the largest open area in the sub. The breech end of the six 30-foot forward torpedo tubes extend 8 feet into the area. Behind the tubes, on racks, are the reload torpedoes. Bunks for the crew are nestled on top of, under, and behind these explosive devices. The forward trim tanks, used to stabilize the sub under water, are located around the torpedo tubes.

In the aft end of the torpedo room is a small hatch which leads to the next compartment. This section has two levels. The upper level is "officer's country," which contains several staterooms for the officers, a shower, a small pantry for snacks, a wardroom for meetings, and a very small office where the ship's paperwork is completed. Beneath this area, separated by a steel deck, is the forward battery room. This space is almost completely filled with 126 batteries, some of which are almost impossible to reach without lying on top of other batteries.

Further aft is the third watertight compartment. Directly through the hatch is the control room. The large wheels which can be used to manually control the diving planes are located on the port side of the room. Above this position is located a large indicator panel which was known as the Christmas tree due to its red and green lights. Each opening in the hull has a light; if a hatch is open, a red light will appear on the board to alert the diving officer. In the center of this area is the helm; it is from this position that the vessel is steered. Behind the

Typical U.S. fleet sub heads out to war with lookouts posted.

helm are ladders leading up to the conning tower and down to the pump room.

To the starboard side of the control room is the radar operator and the plotting table where the executive officer would keep his navigational maps. As mentioned, the pump room is located below the control room. As you might guess, this area is occupied by various pumps and compressors needed to move air and water into and out of the sub. Also located here is a storeroom, the fresh water storage tanks, and the ice machine, a luxury not enjoyed by submariners of other nations.

On the upper deck of the next section is the galley, the crew's mess, a large bunk room, a head, and a washroom. A ladder leads down to a storage area where refrigerated items as well as ammunition, light weapons, and another 126 battery cells are kept.

Nearby, to the aft, we find the first of two compartments containing the diesel engines, the electric generators, and the electric motors.

The upper level of the seventh compartment is occupied by the maneuvering room. Located here are controls necessary to maneuver the ship manually if needed in an emergency. The lower deck is occupied by four large electric motors. The propeller drive shafts are operated by these motors.

The last compartment in the stern of the ship is the after torpedo room. From here the four aft torpedo tubes are operated. Reload torpedoes and crew bunks are also located here.

Back amidships in the control room is a ladder which leads up into the conning tower. It is from the conning tower that the captain will command the sub on all submerged attack actions. In this small cylinder, 8 feet by 14 feet, 11 men will operate and control the attack. The periscope eyepieces are located here as well as sound equipment, the ship intercom equipment, and the Torpedo Data Computer.

Up through a round hatch is the bridge deck. From here the captain will command the vessel during all surface attacks. The TBT, or Target Bearing Transmitter, is mounted on the forward part of the bridge. This device is basically a pair of binoculars mounted to a system which will transmit the direction it is pointed to the officer operating the Torpedo Data

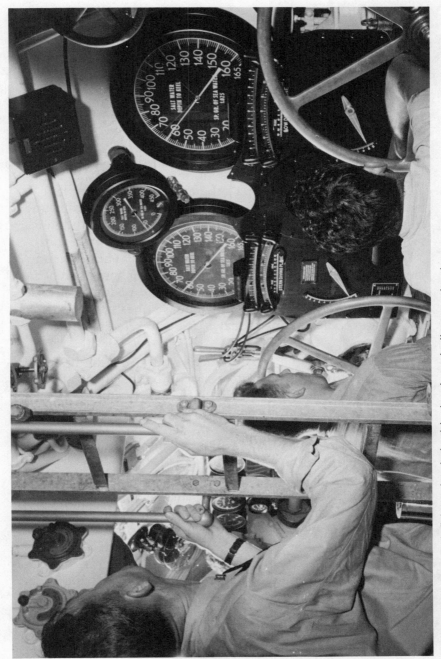

Sub control room and diving wheels. Ladder leads up to the conning tower.

Computer below. Also located here might be an antiaircraft gun. The after section of the bridge, around behind the periscope and antenna assembly, is the fairweather deck; another antiaircraft gun might be mounted here.

Down on the planked main deck is located the heavy gun. Guns on fleet subs were located arbitrarily either fore or aft of the conning tower, and in the later periods of the war, many subs carried guns in both positions.

The Men

Most navies relied on volunteers to man their subs, as did the U.S. Navy. Shipping out in a submarine required a certain temperament, and each job was vitally important to the success of the vessel's missions. This being the case, it did not seem a good idea to force men into subs against their will.

Each sub operated with approximately 55 enlisted men, the vast majority of whom were specialists of some sort. The specialties were motor machinist's mates, torpedomen, electrician's mates, radiomen, signalmen, quartermasters, pharmacist's mate, cooks, gunner's mates, fire controlmen, and a yeoman.

At the start of the war, submarine duty was not highly looked upon, but with the increasing importance and success of submarine operations, the Silent Service rapidly became seen as the fast track for promotions and attracted many of the finest enlisted men and officers.

Graduates of the U.S. Naval Academy made up almost all of the submarine officer personnel when the war started. Shortly thereafter, due to the rapidly expanding force, commanding officers began receiving graduates of the Naval Reserve Officer Training Corps program, or ninety-day wonders as they came to be known. These young officers, although lacking extensive navy background, went on to distinguish themselves throughout the war.

Fleet subs normally carried a complement of five officers; the commander, the executive officer (second-in-command), and three others, each of which took his turn as officer-of-the-deck during one of the three shifts. A smart commander

Crew passes hours playing cards in the tight quarters of the bunk area.

would also carry one or two extra officers to begin the training process, as he knew that any of his current officers could be promoted and move on at any time.

The Submarine Life

Like all warships, submarines must be ready for action 24 hours a day. Subs, therefore, carried enough men to man the necessary posts round-the-clock. Each crew was divided up into three shifts which would operate the ship for 8 hours. For each shift there was an officer assigned as officer-of-the-deck (OOD); the normal operation of the craft was his responsibility during his shift. If an enemy ship was sighted, it was his job to start tracking the ship and remain undetected until the commanding officer could be contacted. Often, once the captain had been notified, he would let the OOD make the initial setup and approach as this could take a number of hours.

It was not uncommon for a sub to go for many days between sightings of enemy shipping. During these slow periods, life aboard the sub would settle down to a regular routine. Studying to take tests in order to qualify for more important posts was a popular pastime as were a number of games such as cribbage and "acey-duecy."

Once a ship was sighted, and the crew was called to battle stations, all signs of boredom rapidly vanished as all hands became involved in the attack. Frequently crew members not directly involved in the operation of the ship during an attack would volunteer to provide extra help either in one of the torpedo rooms or on the bridge as lookouts. On occasion, the captain would provide a running account of how the attack was progressing over the intercom so all crew members would know what was going on. If a hit was scored with a torpedo however, no announcement was necessary as the explosion could be heard throughout the ship.

Life aboard a sub in the process of evading an enemy destroyer was not enjoyed by anyone. Subs were frequently required to remain submerged for 12 hours or more in an effort to sneak slowly away undetected. During these periods all nonessential activity was stopped to conserve the supply of oxygen. Sometimes baking soda was even sprinkled around to absorb the carbon dioxide. If enemy escorts were very close, the air-conditioner compressor might be shut down as well to reduce noise. It is not surprising then that a crew which survived an extended dive and depth-charge attack developed a strong bond which was difficult for new crew members to break through.

The German U-Boat

Under the terms of the Versailles Peace Treaty of 1919, Germany was not allowed to maintain a submarine force. This however did not stop German engineers and technicians from continuing their development and design activities. In 1930, the Germans began developing submarines for other countries. By 1935, when they were once again allowed to operate a sub force, the Germans were ready to begin building a strong U-boat arm as years of design work had already been completed.

The German high command wanted a long-range, fast, quick-diving vessel, which could be quickly and inexpensively manufactured. In 1939, the first of the Type-VIIC craft were delivered and they more than fit the bill. It can be argued that the Type-VIIC U-boat was the best conventional submarine ever built. This ship was designed and built with only fighting in mind, everything else was secondary. They were not built to have a very long life, but it was contended that a war could not possibly last for 20 years (this was the designed life of Allied submarines).

The Type-VIIC vessels were as standardized as possible, which greatly simplified the training process as well as onboard maintenance. The crews were provided with the best supplies that could be found, but when it came to design qualities, habitability was sacrificed to attack and structural considerations.

These ships were of welded single-hull design and possessed a deeper diving capability than their Allied counterparts. This was partially due to the fact that Allied commanders demanded six forward torpedo tubes, and the oval hull shape necessary to accommodate this requirement sacrificed strength. The Germans, however, were willing to live with only four forward torpedo tubes. These tubes could be mounted in a circular hull which was the ideal design shape.

The operational characteristics of the Type-VIIC were a maximum surface speed of 17.6 knots, a maximum submerged speed of 7.6 knots, and a range of 9500 miles. There were four torpedo tubes forward and two aft. They displaced 760 tons on the surface and were 66.5 meters long. This sub had an exceptional crash dive time of less than 30 seconds, close to twice that of a U.S. fleet sub. Another outstanding design feature was the low surface profile. The conning tower was built much lower than that of U.S. subs and although this somewhat limited the distance one could see from the bridge, it made the sub almost invisible on the surface at night.

By the war's end, over 700 of these ships had been built, however only a quarter of them survived.

CHAPTER 3

Lone-Wolf
or
Wolf-Pack

3
Lone-Wolf or Wolf-Pack

The Japanese were quite vulnerable when they started the war in the Pacific. Theirs is a densely populated island nation. They were totally dependent on imports from other countries to support the war effort. The only means of transporting goods into the country was by way of merchant shipping. As long as this shipping was allowed to continue, the war in the Pacific would continue also, but once this shipping was stopped, it was only a matter of time until the Japanese lost. In this sense, the brave men who served in the submarine force have received little of the credit which is due them, for the victory of the U.S. Navy Submarine Force was the decisive element in the war.

A major error was made by the Japanese when they failed to attack the submarine docks in the raid on Pearl Harbor. With the destruction of the fleet, the sub force was left as the only offensive weapon immediately available to use against the Japanese. On the afternoon of December 7, 1941 the order went out, "EXECUTE UNRESTRICTED AIR AND SUBMARINE WARFARE AGAINST JAPAN." This order meant that any Japanese vessels, from fishing boats to destroyers, were fair game for sub attacks.

The prewar training of U.S. sub commanders had not prepared them for all-out war against merchant shipping. Practice attacks had always been made against enemy warships who were aware of their presence, not unsuspecting cargo carriers. Consequently, the first war patrols were notable only by their lack of success. This too was largely due to the unrealistic nature of the prewar training exercises. In these maneuvers, if your sub was "sunk" in action, your career as a naval officer was over. This type of thinking produced a overly cautious group of sub commanders. On top of this, the commanders were ordered to attack from long range, well below periscope depth, using only sound bearings to target the attack. That tactic was tried, but proved to be ineffective.

Early encounters with Japanese escorts showed that the U.S had an exaggerated view of the effectiveness of these ships. Escorts were not sent with all convoys, as expected, so many ships were traveling unprotected. Also, when enemy escorts were present, they were not as dangerous as previously thought. The Japanese escorts were not aware of how deep the U.S. subs could dive, and, as a result, they set their depth-charges too high up. Also, the commanders of these enemy escorts also had a tendency to overestimate their own effectiveness, cutting short an attack on the slightest evidence that the sub had been destroyed.

As the war progressed a new breed of young and aggressive sub commander came into the service. Many of these men dared to depart from the established theories of attack and devised new and effective techniques. They would spend hours examining the patrol reports of other subs trying to find a new tactic which might have a higher probability for success in a given situation.

With very few boats to work with at the beginning of the war, the use of wolf-pack tactics was not an option available to the U.S. high command. Even if this had been possible, it is not likely that pack tactics would have been widely used. The U.S. sub commanders were too individualistic and competitive to work closely together. They were at their best when given a territory to patrol and left to their own resourcefulness in deciding the best way to accomplish their task. For the most part this was how the sub war was conducted.

A commander was given orders to patrol a specific area of the Pacific. Occasionally, intelligence information regarding the location of enemy shipping was available; in such instances, a radio message—or Ultra—was sent to the closest ship. Later in the war, pack tactics were used to some extent but usually with small groups of two or three subs. Even then, the various commanders would compete for the best patrolling

Lookouts below. Conning tower lookouts scramble to get below once the order to dive is given.

station or post. They had to be very careful in this circum-
stance as Japanese subs were also operating in these waters,
and a commander could easily be fooled into thinking the enemy sub was one of his pack-mates.

Postwar analysis showed the U.S. sub commander to be
most dangerous and effective when working alone in an area
and given only the broadest of orders.

The U-Boat War

The U.S. was forced into the war unexpectedly by the attack
on Pearl Harbor. The Germans, however, did not have such a
good excuse for starting the war with an extremely small sub
force. Yet, when they started the war, they had only 22
long-range U-boats to operate in the Atlantic. In 1938, the
commander of the U-boat fleet, Captain Doenitz, had pro-
posed a brilliant plan for a 300-U-boat fleet, this would have
allowed for 100 ships to be in refitting, 100 to be on patrol,
and 100 to be en route at all times. Hitler, however, was taken
with the size and power of battleships, so very little shipyard
time could be spared for subs.

Doenitz had a more advanced view of sub warfare than
his Allied counterparts. He put little emphasis on attacking naval warships. He felt that the small chance of success did not
justify the risk. All of the U-boat effort went to stop the convoy action between the U.S. and Great Britain. In this effort,
they were extremely successful. In the first nine months of the
war, U-boats sank 300 ships totalling 1,137,000 tons; later
they would be sinking almost 1,000,000 tons a month.

The German tactics were relatively simple, Doenitz fa-
vored concentration over surprise. Intelligence reports would
allow him to position a large number of U-boats along a convoy's route; then they would wait for dark. In the cover of
darkness, they would penetrate the escort defense and take
position within the convoy on the surface. Once in position,
they could pick their targets at leisure. Almost all of their attacks were conducted from the surface and from very short
range, often only a few hundred yards. In this situation, each
captain acted independently so collisions with other subs did
occasionally occur.

The U-boat commanders continued to enjoy this success through 1942. Then in May of 1943, the tide turned when the Allies began using carrier-based air cover, new improved radar equipment, and improved antisubmarine tactics. This forced the German subs to change tactics and start conducting mostly submerged attacks which greatly reduced their effectiveness. The Germans never could catch up with the Allied technology and thereafter lost subs faster than they could be replaced. Once the Allies were allowed to operate successful convoys, the war in the Atlantic was all but over.

CHAPTER 4

Submarine Attack

4
Submarine Attack

"Up scope. I want to check for enemy air cover before we get too close." The captain squatted down to meet the eyepiece as the periscope slid up from the well. The eyepiece stopped two feet from the floor. The captain slapped the handles down and hopped quickly around in a circle as he surveyed the horizon. Seeing no aircraft, he signaled for the scope to be raised to its full height and lined up the crosshairs on the target they had been stalking for the last hour, a large tanker.

"Main target. Bearing . . . mark! Range . . . mark! Down scope!" The whole process had taken only seven seconds.

"What's the range?"

"One zero two zero zero yards, sir."

"Distance to target track?"

"Four zero one zero yards," replied the executive officer who was staring intently at the whirring dials of the Torpedo Data Computer. "Ten minutes since last zig, sir," he added, anticipating the captain's next question.

They both knew the situation was less than perfect; they had barely managed to catch up to the convoy when it had made a large zig away from them. There was no sign that they had been spotted; it just must have been a regular zigzag intended to make the convoy's actual course and destination hard to detect. Now, unless the target made a zig back toward them, they would be forced to take an extremely long-range shot or start the approach all over again.

The captain squeezed through the crowded conning tower and stood behind the young sonarman. If the convoy made a change in course, he would be the first to know.

"Time since last look?"

"One minute-thirty, sir."

The soundman broke in, "Change in screw speed, sir.

They're making a turn!"

"Up scope!" ordered the captain as he made his way back toward the center of the tower. The exec had the scope up and pointing to the correct bearing by the time he got there.

"They're zigging toward us. Down scope. I'll give them another minute to finish the turn. The escort was about 20 degrees ahead of the tanker and slightly to port." The whirring of the TDC motors made the only sound as they waited for the seconds to pass.

"One minute, sir."

"Up scope. Bearing . . . mark! Range . . . mark! Down scope." The skipper slapped the handles up and stepped back toward the plotting table. "New angle-on-the-bow is port 20, looks like she's coming right down the track. What's the distance to the new track?"

"One zero zero zero yards, sir."

The captain would have liked to set up for a stern shot, but there was no time for that now.

"Up attack scope." Scope number 2 slid up toward the captain's waiting hands. "Bearing . . . mark. Down scope. Speed looks good at ten knots. The escort, looks like an old destroyer. It's on the far side of the tanker. How does that speed check with the TDC?"

"Speed checks good at ten knots. Range is one four zero zero yards."

"We'll fire on this observation. Shoot three with a two-degree spread. Up scope." Once again, the captain lined up the crosshairs on the center of the tanker. "Bearing . . . mark!"

"Good TDC firing solution, captain," said the exec who was still manning the Torpedo Data Computer.

"Fire! Down scope."

The sub shuddered as each of the three torpedoes left their tubes.

"All three torpedoes fired electrically."

"Torpedoes running hot, straight, and normal," reported the soundman.

"Fifteen seconds to impact for number 1, sir."

"Up scope."

"Three . . . two . . . one. . . . Number 1 is a miss." The

Captain at periscope.

disappointment was only momentary as the whole sub shook with impact of the second and, shortly thereafter, third torpedoes. The captain reported that the tanker had been hit amidships and aft and was sinking by the stern.

Attack Basics

Obtaining a favorable position from which to fire your torpedoes is no accident. You are required to solve a number of complex problems, often with limited information. One of the first things you will have to determine, once a convoy is sighted, is the direction of travel or heading.

To accomplish this, steer the sub directly at the target and then, over a period of time, note the relative motion of the target. If the target is moving to your left or right, then you have determined which direction to steer to intercept the convoy. If the target does not move at all, or moves very slightly, then the target is either heading directly toward you or away from you. In this case, maintain your heading for a couple of minutes; if you don't notice a decrease in range, then they are probably heading away from you, and you have a long end-around approach in store.

–·–·–·– **Line of Sight**

·········· **Path of Torpedo**

———— **Path of Ship or Sub**
on Surface

— — — — — **Path of Sub Submerged**

◁══⊜▷ **Submarine**

⊣▢◻▣▢⊢▷ **Armed Escort**

▢◻▢▣▢▷ **Convoy Ship**

Drawing Legend

The Standard Approach

Once you have determined the target heading, your next step, generally, is to obtain a position ahead of the target and just off of the target track. As a rule of thumb, the best approach, once you pull ahead of the target, is accomplished by taking a heading which is 90 degrees from the line of sight of the target. This tactic may be used submerged or on the surface, and there are an infinite number of variations to this tactic. However, this maneuvering plan will be the base for all attempts to intersect the course of a moving target.

During the approach phase, you must be alert at all times since the situation can change very quickly. You should also make an attempt during this period to determine the following:

• The number and type of escorts, if any
• The zigzag pattern and base course
• The number and types of ships

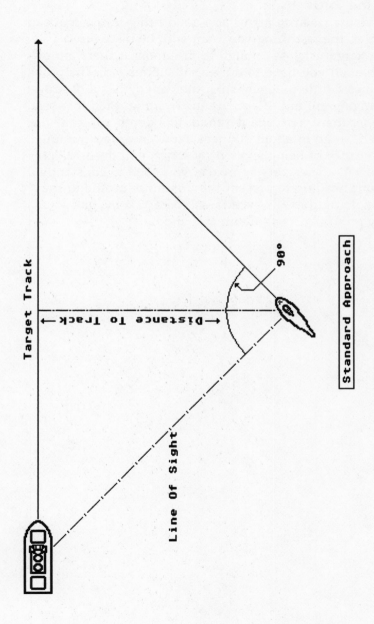

Target Track

Distance To Track

90°

Line Of Sight

Standard Approach

Pointing the Target

If you have managed to arrive at a good firing position ahead of the target, the last thing you want is to be discovered before the target is close enough to fire upon. If there are no escorts, then all you have to do is wait submerged. The problem becomes a little tougher when the convoy has a destroyer or two hanging around. If you are just waiting, then it is best to be deeper than periscope depth; at this depth you can still be rammed, so go to about 100 feet. Now, in order to minimize the chance of being spotted by sonar, you need to "point the target." As the escorts approach, you need to constantly change your heading to present the minimum profile to the enemy. By doing this, the escorts will pass you by, and you can safely go to periscope depth and shoot.

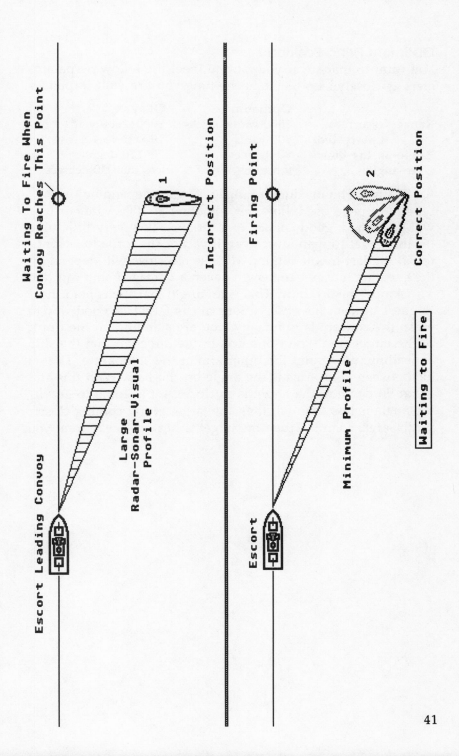

Waiting To Fire When
Convoy Reaches This Point

Incorrect Position

Firing Point

Correct Position

1

2

Escort Leading Convoy

Large
Radar—Sonar—Visual
Profile

Escort

Minimum Profile

Waiting to Fire

Optimum Firing Position

You want to maneuver your sub to meet the following parameters as closely as possible at the time you fire your torpedoes:

	Optimum	Okay
Range: (escorted)	1000 yards or less	1000–2000 yards
(unescorted)	500 yards	1000 or less
Angle-on-the-bow:	90 degrees	70–110 degrees
Gyro angle:	0 degrees	less than 30 degrees

Range. The maximum range will vary depending on the type of torpedo used; however, shooting at 1000 yards or less will give you a good chance of a hit and allow very little time for the target to maneuver even if you or the torpedo is spotted at the last moment. How close is too close will depend on the situation, but remember that even a damaged ship can ram.

Angle-on-the-bow. This is an angle that the captain has to guess at from his observations of the target. A good way to grasp the concept is to imagine you are standing on the front of the target ship. Point one arm in the direction that the ship is heading, now point the other arm at the submarine. The angle between your arms is the angle-on-the-bow. With this angle at 90 degrees, the target is as close as it is going to get. If the angle is less than 90, then the target is still coming closer; if it is larger than 90, then the target is heading away from you.

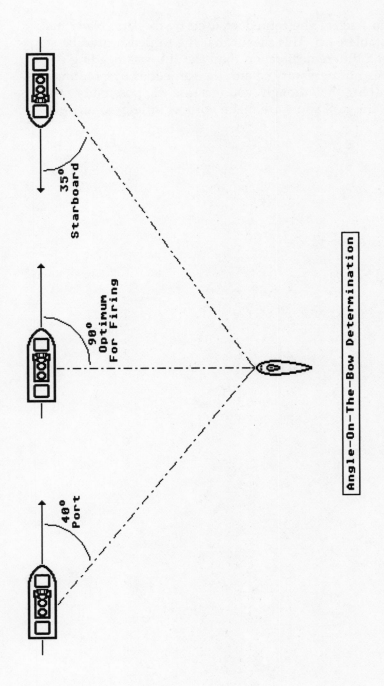

35°
Starboard

90°
Optimum
For Firing

40°
Port

Angle-On-The-Bow Determination

43

Gyro Angle. The torpedoes used by the U.S. Navy had an adjustable gyro. This meant that the torpedo could be set to run in a different direction than the sub was heading so that it was not necessary to aim the torpedoes by pointing the sub. By doing this, though, you increase the possibility of an error, so the best shots are made with as little gyro angle as possible.

Submarine Attack

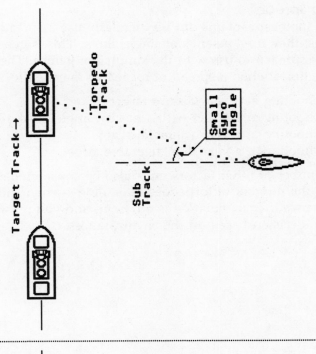

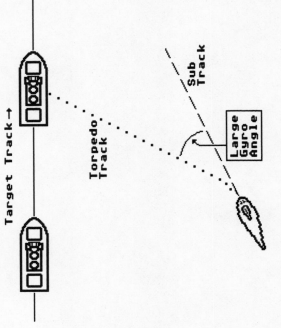

Torpedo Spread

Many of the best captains did not regularly use a spread of torpedoes; they fired a series of single shots. This is generally the best approach to use with the simulation games. There are, however, times when a spread of torpedoes is called for:

- When shooting at a very distant target
- When shooting at a target with a narrow angle-on-the-bow
- When shooting at a very valuable target
- When shooting at a very maneuverable target

A number of other factors must also be considered—for instance, the number of torpedoes remaining—when choosing to fire a spread. Each situation is different, and you must make your own decision based on the circumstances.

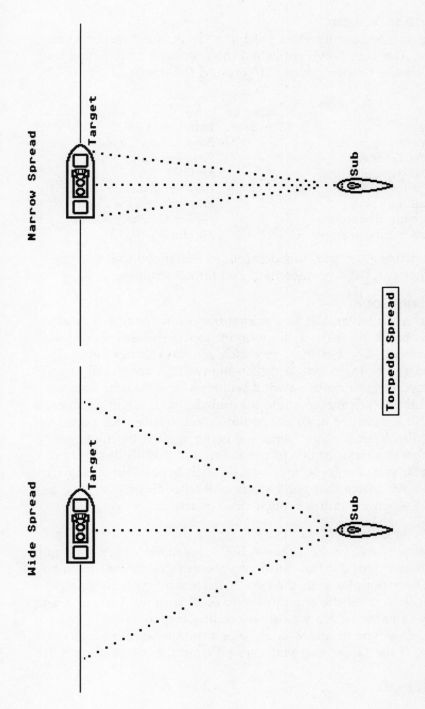

Torpedo Volume

The number of torpedoes fired at a target is the torpedo volume. The U.S. Navy published the following table listing the volume of fire for various targets and the points of aim to be used.

Target	Number of Torpedoes	Points of Aim
Battleships, cruisers	4	Bow, forward, mid, aft
Aircraft carrier	4	Bow, forward, middle, aft
Small cruisers	1	Middle
Large transports	3	Forward mid, mid, aftermid
Small transports	2	Fireroom, engine room
Large merchant ships	2	Forward middle, middle
Small merchant ships	1	Middle

During the war, this doctrine was changed to reflect a higher emphasis on merchant and tanker shipping.

Twilight Zone

Your main advantage as a submarine commander is that of invisibility. As such, it is important to use this advantage with great skill. The best time to attack, all other things being equal, is during dawn or dusk—the twilight hours. An attack carried out during this period will make the most of your invisibility advantage while maximizing your target's vulnerability. A dawn or dusk attack allows you to use your periscope; yet the chances of the periscope being spotted by the target are greatly reduced due to the fading light. With this style of attack, you can get in much closer than is possible during daylight. Also note that good sonar avoidance technique must be used when operating at such close quarters.

Gun Attacks

Due to its narrow beam the sub did not make a very good gun platform. This did not, however, prevent gun actions from being very popular with the crew. Gun attacks gave them a chance to meet the enemy face-to-face, with all the sound and fury of battle which was absent during torpedo attacks.

This type of attack does have a number of drawbacks. First, if the target is armed, one hit from the target's gun will

Gun action aboard the USS *Silversides*.

likely cause much more damage than one hit from your gun; in fact one hit from an enemy gun could prevent you from diving and eventually prove fatal. Second, unless the target has already been damaged by a torpedo hit, it is very difficult to sink a ship with the gun. Third, the guns used on subs were just not very accurate. Keeping those caveats in mind, the gun can be very useful in sinking damaged unarmed merchant ships and as a last resort against escorts when you cannot submerge.

Periscope Technique

During the approach and attack, it is imperative that you remain undetected. Using proper periscope techniques will improve your chances of success. Keep the following tips in mind whenever you raise the scope:

- Keep your looks as short as possible.
- Reduce your speed to below 3 knots before raising the scope.
- Don't leave the scope up to watch the torpedoes hit unless you are not threatened by escorts.
- Don't stay at periscope depth unless you are going to use the scope soon. You can be rammed at this depth.
- Use the scope from the maximum depth allowable. This will keep to a minimum the amount of the scope out of the water.

Convoy Zigzags

Frequently a convoy will attempt to hide its true course by zigging and zagging back and forth across its base course. It is often necessary to observe a convoy for a period of time to determine its base course; once this has been established, you can make your end-around approach on the proper heading. When attacking a zigging convoy, it is best to shoot as soon as possible after a zig to prevent unanticipated course changes after you have fired your torpedoes.

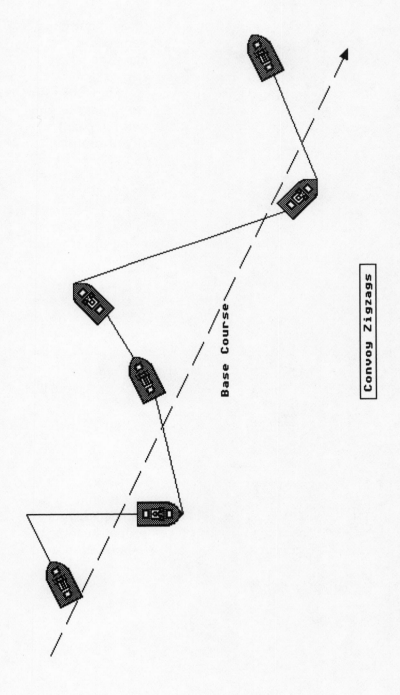

Base Course

Convoy Zigzags

CHAPTER 5

Attack Tactics

Jokuja Maru heading for the bottom after being torpedoed by the USS *Aspro*, May, 1944 as seen through periscope.

5
Attack Tactics

Once a convoy is sighted and you begin your approach, things start to happen very quickly. That is why you need to have a good plan right from the start. That is also why you need to be well versed in a number of different attack techniques because things can, and often do, change.

What follows is a description of a number of different plans for attack. As situations change, some of these tactics will lead logically to other tactics. Take the time to become familiar with all of them. Sooner or later you'll need each one.

Daylight Submerged Attack
Situation: Day or Twilight
You spot a target behind you. All you must do is maneuver close to the target, track, and shoot.

1. The target is sighted. You determine that it is heading toward you. Begin a standard approach to the target track. Once you get close to visual range, submerge to 100 feet.
2. Continue to track the target and establish a position close to the target track. Maintain a minimum profile.
3. When the target reaches a good firing position go up to periscope depth and shoot.

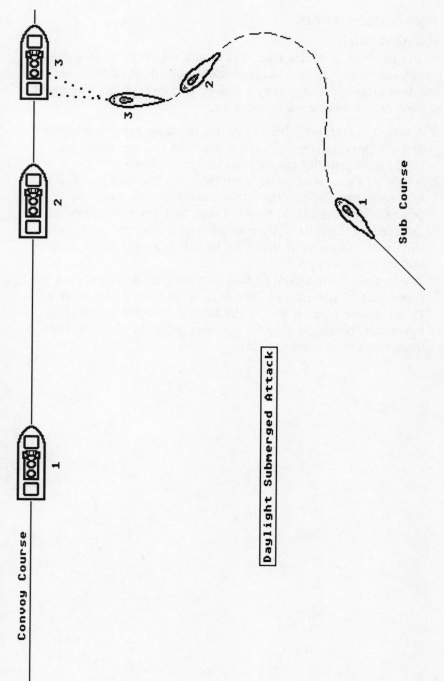

Convoy Course

Sub Course

Daylight Submerged Attack

Night Surface Attack

Situation: Night

At the beginning of the war, this attack was not in the book, but as sub commanders became more confident of their ability and less afraid of the enemy's ability to detect them, the night surface attack became a favorite tactic.

1. A target is sighted which is either heading away from you or on a parallel course. Take a position just outside visual range on a parallel course. Go to flank speed.
2. While you are passing the convoy, note the number and movement of the escorts. Make sure that you maintain a position beyond visual range. Once you are well ahead of the convoy, turn back sharply toward it and reduce speed (this will reduce your visibility to the enemy). Again, maintain a minimum profile.
3. Try to time your attack so that the escorts, if any, are on the other side of the convoy. Move in to at least 1000 yards and shoot. Remember, if you maintain a minimum profile and approach the target slowly, you can get a lot closer at night than you can during the day.

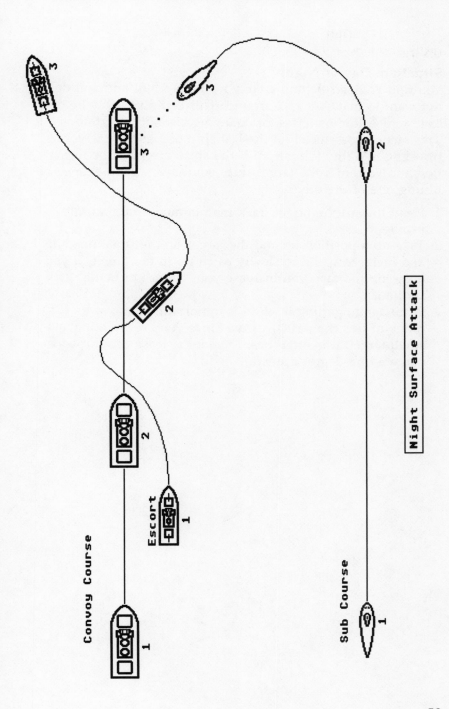

Convoy Course

Escort

Night Surface Attack

Sub Course

Up-the-Kilt Shot

Situation: Day or Night

You find yourself behind a convoy, undetected, and you do not want to make an end-around. This could possibly be due to low fuel, low batteries, or changing visibility conditions. This tactic is best used on the last ship of a convoy which is traveling in a line formation. If the ships are in a line formation and you miss the target ship, you have a good chance of hitting one of the other ships.

1. Head toward the target track maintaining a minimum profile.
2. Take up a position behind the target on the same heading and increase speed to slowly catch up to the target. If you come up too fast, you increase your chance of being spotted.
3. Once again, getting in close is important, so move to a range of less than 1000 yards. Since you are shooting at a small target, it is often best to shoot at least two torpedoes using a one-degree spread.

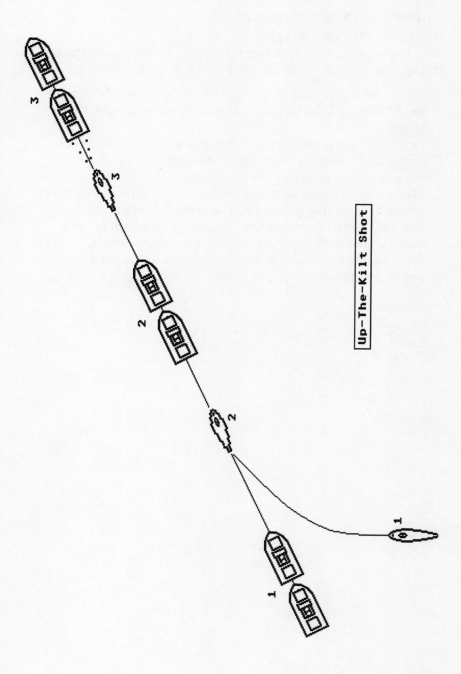

Up-The-Kilt Shot

Daylight Surface End-Around
Situation: Day or Twilight
This is probably the most commonly used maneuver. Master it, and you should begin to see a lot of ships go down.

1. You have a contact but you are too far away to determine the heading of the target. Submerge and head toward the target.
2. Once you are close enough, determine the convoy speed, range, and heading. Remain submerged and head back out beyond visual range.
3. When you get beyond visual range, surface and order flank speed on a course parallel to the target course.
4. Get well ahead of the target, submerge to 100 feet, and make a standard approach with a minimum profile.
5. Once you are within shooting range, go up to periscope depth and shoot.

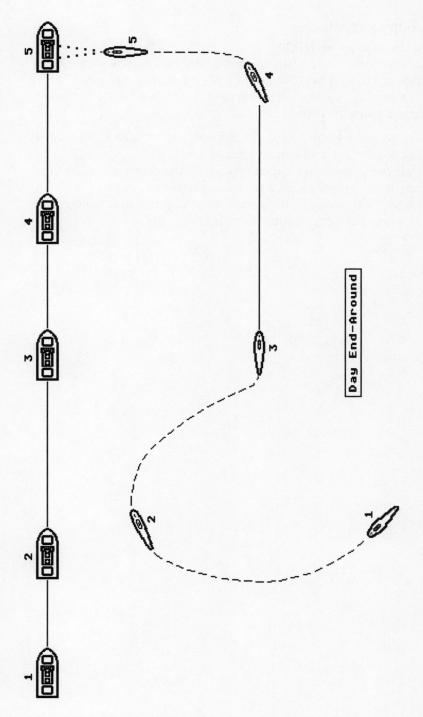

Day End-Around

Pop-Up Gun Attack

Situation: Day or Night

You have disabled a ship so that it can move only very slowly or not at all, and you want to finish it off with the gun. A clever enemy captain keeps turning the ship so as to show you only a minimum profile for your gun attack.

1. Try to get a good firing position on the surface as the target keeps turning away from you.
2. Submerge to a safe depth (you may need to pass right beneath the target so give yourself plenty of room).
3. Move so the ship is broadside to you and surface. Be ready to start shooting as soon as you come up.

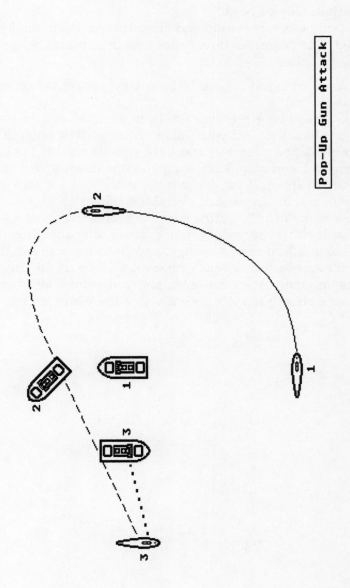

Down-the-Throat Shot

Situation: Day or Night

This tactic was rarely used and almost never intentionally employed. The down-the-throat shot usually represented a change in plans.

1. You are trying to approach the enemy undetected on an end-around.
2. You realize your presence has been detected and an enemy escort heads toward you. Submerge to periscope depth, if the periscope is usable, and head directly toward the oncoming escort ship. Keep the periscope down until you are ready to shoot. If you leave it up, it may get hit with enemy gunfire, and you wouldn't be able to shoot at all.
3. At a range of 1500 yards, raise the scope and shoot a spread of at least two torpedoes. Immediately after shooting, dive, make a radical course change, and go to flank speed. If you don't score a hit, be ready for a rough time. If the convoy has only one escort, however, and you score a hit, then you have a chance to systematically sink the whole group.

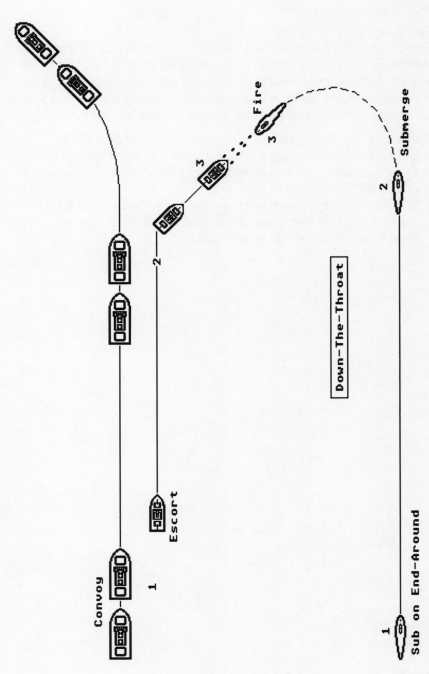

Convoy

Escort

1

2

3

Fire

Submerge

Down-The-Throat

Sub on End-Around

The Waiting Ambush

Situation: Day or Night

Sometimes you get just plain lucky. You spot a target, plot its
course, and find that the target is heading right down the track
to you. All you need to do is hide and wait. Be careful, however. Even in the simplest setups, things must be done with
precision or you could go from hunter to hunted very quickly.

1. The convoy is spotted heading in your basic direction.
2. Submerge and take up a position just off the target track.
   Once you are in position, maintain a minimum profile and a
   depth of 100 feet or more.
3. As the target approaches at an angle-on-the-bow of 90 degrees, go up to periscope depth and shoot when the escorts,
   if any, are as far away as possible.

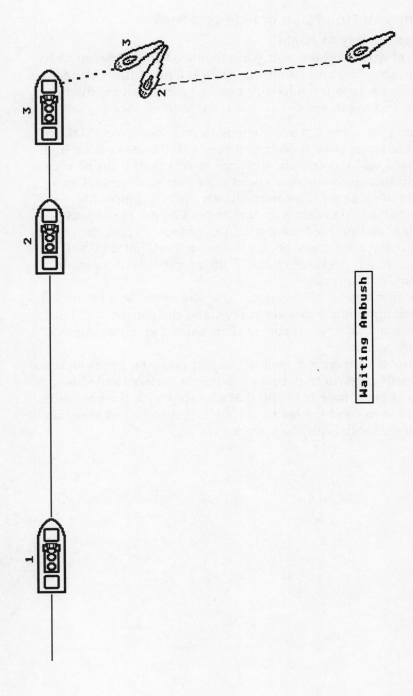

Waiting Ambush

Intentional Escort Lure or Hide-and-Seek
Situation: Day or Night

As you gain confidence in your abilities, you may want to try more advanced and dangerous tactics. One of these dangerous maneuvers is to intentionally expose your presence, then go deep, and sneak inside the escort for a quick shot.

1. You spot a good size convoy with only one escort. Take a standard approach on the surface at full speed (using high speed will increase the distance at which you can be seen and increase your dive speed once you submerge). Once you are sighted, dive immediately and cut power to one-third. Maintain a minimum profile, get as deep as possible, and proceed on toward the convoy. Expect the convoy to make a zig away once you are spotted, but they will resume their previous course if the escort cannot maintain contact with you.

2. By this time, if all has gone well, the escort will be busy looking where you were earlier, and the convoy will have resumed its original course. This should give you a good approach angle.

3. Now the escort is hopelessly out of position, get as close as possible, go up to periscope depth or surface, and shoot. A good tactic here is to shoot at one ship with the bow tubes and then continue on across the target track and shoot at another ship with the stern tubes.

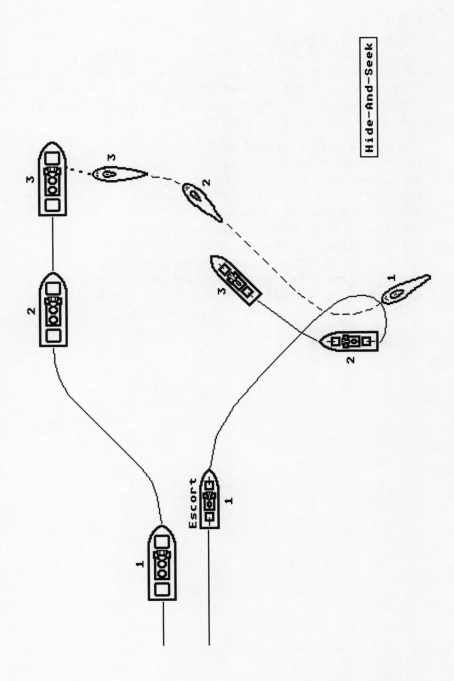

Hide-And-Seek

Escort

The Spinner

Situation: Day or Night

In some simulations and situations, you may find that you have a surface-speed advantage over the escort traveling with the convoy. A good sub commander will seek to exploit any advantage available. This tactic will use this speed difference to lure the escort into a bad position.

1. You have a convoy spotted, and you move into visual range. An escort moves out to intercept you.
2. As the escort moves out to intercept you, start to turn away from the convoy. Since the escort is heading on an intercept course it will head in a direction in front of you. Once the escort is out in front of you continue the turn so that you are heading back toward the convoy. At this point it is a race back to the convoy. Due to your speed and position advantages (gained by your spin), you should win this race.
3. Once you close to firing range, shoot your torpedoes while maintaining full speed. Head on across the target track and shoot stern tubes if possible. Continue on to make your escape on the surface.

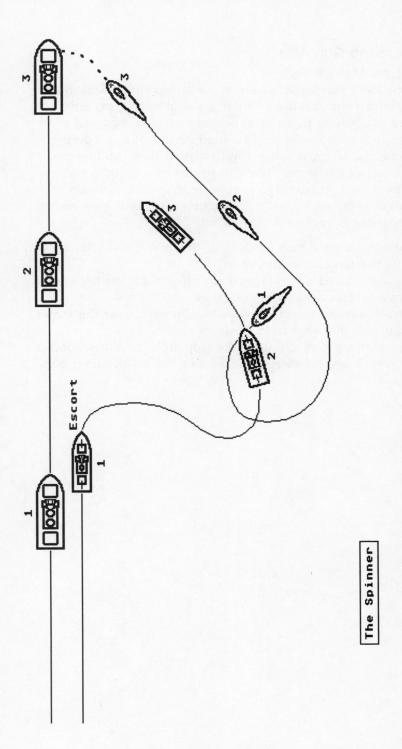

The Spinner

The Running Gun Attack
Situation: Day or Night

The situation may arise where you want to sink a fast-moving target with your gun only. Sinking a ship with guns only will require many hits. In order to accomplish this, you will need to engage the target for an extended period of time; during this time the target is not going to just sit there and let you blast it out of the water. You will need to use your speed and maneuverability advantage to repeatedly gain a position where the target is broadside to your position. This will give you the best possible chance of scoring a hit.

1. You have a good gun position at this point, but after several shots the target turns away.
2. Use your speed advantage to cut off the target's turn and gain a favorable shooting position.
3. Once again the target turns away. Outmaneuver the target again and shoot when in position.
4. Repeat this procedure until the ship sinks or slows enough for you to use submerged pop-up tactics for the final blow.

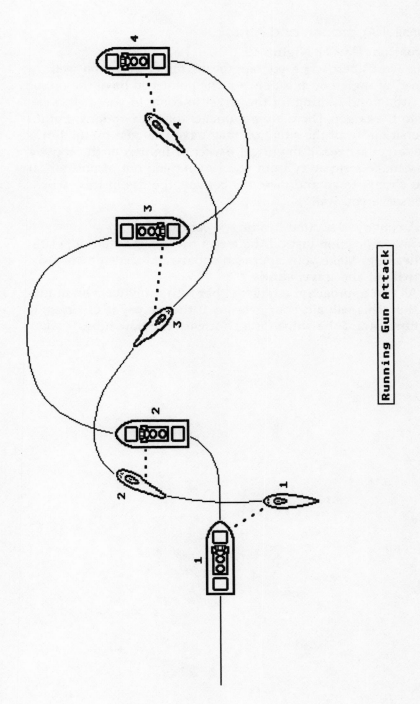

Running Gun Attack

Parallel Approach and Attack
Situation: Day or Night

This works best when you are on the target track and well ahead of the target position. At this point you have the option of sitting and waiting for the target to come to you or you can go to the target. There are arguments for both options, but if you sit and wait the situation may have changed by the time the target arrives, it might get darker or lighter, or the convoy may make a zig away from you leaving you out of position. If you choose to go and meet the convoy, the use of this tactic will serve you well.

1. A convoy is spotted heading toward you.
2. Take a position just off the target track and on an opposite heading. Make your approach submerged if it's daytime or twilight and travel slowly.
3. As you approach the target either turn away for a stern tube shot (this will aid your getaway if the convoy is escorted) or turn toward the ships for a shot with the bow tubes.

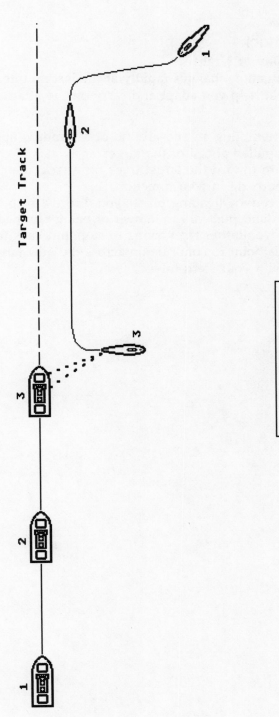

Target Track

Parallel Approach

Crossing Attack

Situation: Day or Night

When the situation changes rapidly at the last minute, using this tactic will help you adapt and carry on the attack with success.

1. You are attempting an end-around or a standard approach. You have pulled ahead of the target.
2. As you turn toward the target track for attack, the convoy takes a sharp zig in your direction.
3. This new convoy heading places you directly in the convoy's path and puts you in danger of being rammed if you do not move. Rather than trying to stop and back up, it is best at this point to continue on across the new target track and fire with your stern tubes.

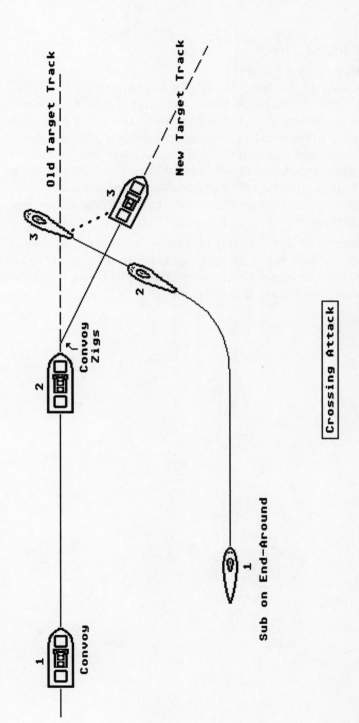

Old Target Track

New Target Track

3

3

Convoy Zigs

2

2

Sub on End-Around

1

Convoy

1

Crossing Attack

Deep Sound Attack

Situation: Day or Night

At the start of the war, the deep sound attack was the preferred tactic of the Navy high command. They felt that exposing the scope was an unnecessary risk. The advent of sonar had made them overly cautious. In actuality, this tactic was rarely used and had a limited success. There are times, however, when this tactic can be useful, and it is a challenge to see if you can pull it off with only sonar information. You might want to take a shot at a destroyer circling above you using this tactic.

1. A convoy is sighted, and you begin a standard approach.
2. Once you reach visual range, submerge to at least 100 feet.
3. Move in close and shoot from this depth using range and position data from the sonar.

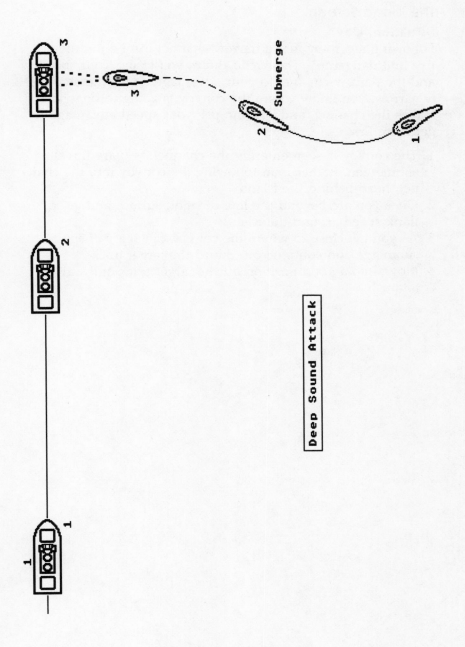

Deep Sound Attack

The Island Screen

Situation: Day

Following a convoy into a narrow channel can be unproductive and dangerous. This tactic allows you to use your speed and the narrow channel to your advantage. Since the channel is narrow, you know where the convoy is going to be when it leaves the channel, and you can use your speed advantage to get there first.

1. The convoy is seen entering the channel; you are traveling submerged. Rather than following the convoy into the channel, head behind the island.
2. Once you are beyond the line of sight, surface and go to flank speed around the island.
3. As you get close to where the convoy can see you again, submerge and continue on toward the target track.
4. Move into a good position off the target track and wait in ambush.

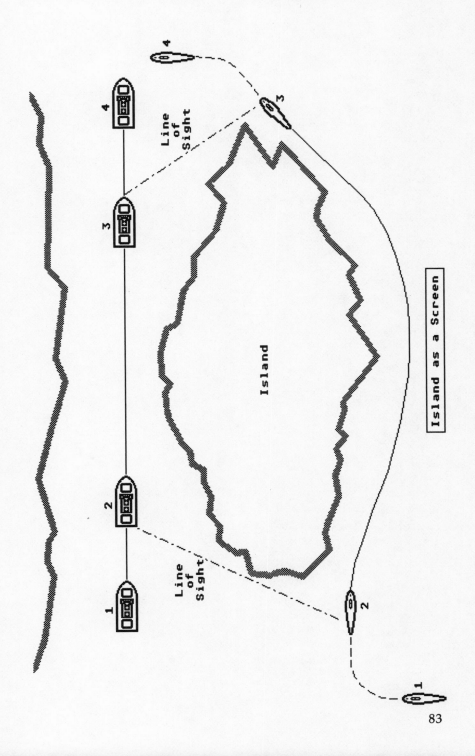

Island

Line of Sight

Line of Sight

Island as a Screen

CHAPTER 6

Pull the Plug
and
Take 'er Deep

6
Pull the Plug and
Take 'er Deep

As the burning tanker slid slowly beneath the surface, leaving only a fiery oil slick, the sub commander barked a list of orders to the control-room crew.

"Make your depth 400 feet, all ahead full, full left rudder!"

"High-speed screws, sir. No change in sonar activity, though. I don't think they've found us yet," reported the sonar operator.

Above, the old Japanese destroyer was pouring on the oil in order to pick up speed. Now furious at the loss of her charge, the destroyer was milling about desperately trying to locate the source of the deadly torpedo attack. Meanwhile the sub sought the safety of deep water.

"Increase in sonar, I think they've got us, sir!"

The captain swore under his breath. He knew that turning away from the enemy as he did would present a larger sonar profile, but if he could have made it without detection, he would have had no trouble slipping quietly away.

"O.K., let's rig for depth charges. All engines stop, rudder amidships, and rig for silent running."

Systems all over the boat were shut down and all hands not directly involved with the operation of the boat went to their bunks and looked for something to hang onto. The captain watched as the depth indicator passed 150 feet.

"They're gearing up for a run, heading straight toward us." The crew listened silently as the high-speed screws got closer and louder. At only 175 feet, this could be trouble. The destroyer passed overhead and shortly thereafter the charges were heard to hit the water.

Boom! Boom! Boom! The boat rocked violently as the depth charges exploded overhead. Once again the Japanese had set their charges to explode too high in the water. But not by much.

"Forward torpedo room here," a voice came over the intercom. "We're taking on water from the hatch, sir, but we've got the block-and-tackle out, and I think we can control it."

The captain sent the exec forward to check it out. The last thing he needed in a critical situation was a nose-heavy ship.

"Depth 225 feet, sir. Water temp dropping."

At last a bit of luck. They were passing through a thermocline; enemy sonar would have a difficult time finding them now.

"All ahead one-third. Full right rudder."

Again the destroyer passed overhead and dropped charges, this time off the port side and not quite as close.

"Depth 400 feet, sir." Finally.

"Forward torpedo room."

"Yes, sir, forward torp room here."

"What's the situation up there?"

"Not too bad. We've got the hatch tied down and slowed the leak," replied the exec. The destroyer dropped again this time even further away.

"Maintain this depth, rudder amidships. Looks like we're going to make it."

The sound of distant explosions continued for the next hour as the angry destroyer tried in vain to locate the silent killer which was slowly slipping away.

Defensive Tactics and Strategies

Sinking that big transport doesn't do you any good if you get your hull caved in by an escort shortly thereafter. The following ideas and tactics will help you live to hunt another day and sail back to the base with your tubes empty and the broom tied to the mast, a clean sweep.

Your plans for escape and withdrawal should begin with your initial attack and approach plans. The attack should be planned so that not only do you fire from a position where you have a good chance of scoring a hit, but from which you

Dive! Sub heads for deep water.

also have a good chance of getting away safely. When planning your approach, keep the following ideas in mind.

The Type and Number of Escorts

Early in the war, many of the convoys traveled unescorted; later some convoys were escorted by two or three destroyers. Finding out the number of escorts will have a major impact on your attack and defensive plans.

A convoy with only one escort can be attacked from the weak side, the side without escort protection. Under these circumstances, a shot can be taken from a much closer range than if the convoy had two escorts. Also it would be necessary to leave damaged stragglers behind with no escort if there were only one destroyer. Hiding submerged from multiple escorts is also more difficult due to the problem of presenting a minimum profile at all times to two or more ships. In some cases it may be wise simply not to attack heavily escorted convoys.

Control room of the USS *Wahoo* as they sit out depth-charge attack.

Depth of the Water

This is of major importance as the ability to hide underwater is the sub's big advantage. Shallow water reduces this advantage. When an attack is planned in shallow water, it is best to wait until twilight or dark when an escape can be made on the surface if necessary.

When forced to dive in shallow water, make sure you know where the bottom is; grounding the sub while being hunted can prove fatal. If you are being hunted in shallow water, you should use the tighter turning radius of the sub and even reverse speed, if needed, to keep the destroyer from getting right over you. Each time the escort passes by, try and work your way closer to deep water. Then, if it's possible, make a dash, keeping close to the bottom.

If all else fails, rig for silent running, sit on the bottom, and hope for the best.

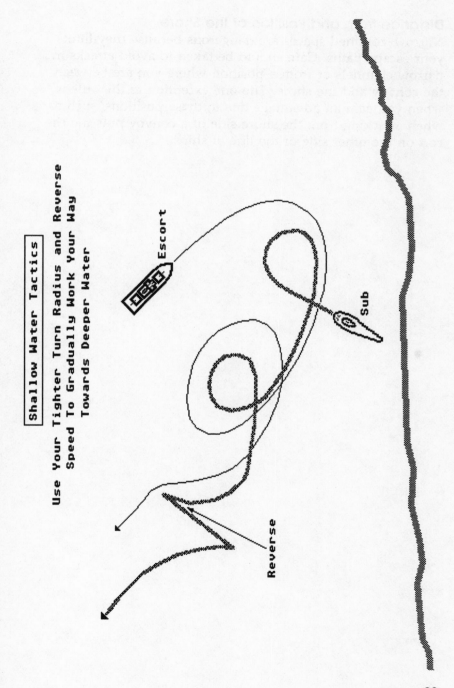

Shallow Water Tactics

Use Your Tighter Turn Radius and Reverse
Speed To Gradually Work Your Way
Towards Deeper Water

Escort

Sub

Reverse

Distance from and Position of the Shore

Narrow, confined spaces are dangerous because they limit your escape paths. Care should be taken to avoid attacks in narrow channels or from a position where you are between the convoy and the shore. The one exception to this rule is when you gain an advantage due to these positions, such as when attacking from the shore side of a convoy puts the escort on the other side of the line of ships.

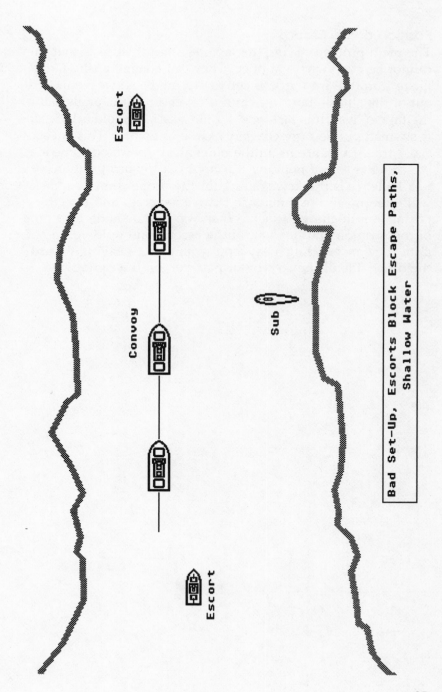

Bad Set-Up, Escorts Block Escape Paths, Shallow Water

CHAPTER 6

Position of the Escorts

The main problem facing the Japanese escort ships is that they cannot be everywhere at once. They can change position, move from the front of the convoy to the back, weave in and out of the ships—but they cannot cover all of the angles all of the time. Given this fact, you should work to avoid attack tactics which put you unnecessarily close to escorts. This is especially true if you are using the older steam-powered torpedoes which leave a trail pointing directly back to your position.

Patience is the key. Waiting for the proper time to attack will often mean the difference between success and a teeth-jarring, depth-charge attack. When waiting to shoot, take note of the position and heading of the escorts and hold your shot until they are heading away from you, either heading toward the other side of the convoy or past you on the same side.

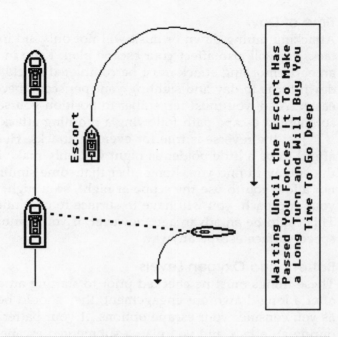

Waiting Until the Escort Has Passed You Forces It To Make a Long Turn and Will Buy You Time To Go Deep

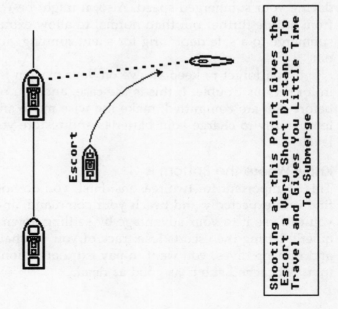

Shooting at this Point Gives the Escort a Very Short Distance To Travel and Gives You Little Time To Submerge

Time of Day

Attacking during dawn or dusk will not only aid in your attack, but will also affect your escape plan. Keep in mind that an early-morning attack must be completed quickly before dawn turns to day and sighting your periscope becomes much easier. Also, you must remember to position yourself for a submerged escape path following a morning attack.

Just the reverse is true for evening attacks. Here you can afford to be a little bolder as night will only make it harder for the enemy to find you. Remember that some simulations will not allow you to use the scope at night, so if night falls during your approach, you will have to surface to continue the attack. This could be an advantage, however, if you planned a high-speed surface escape anyway.

Battery and Oxygen Levels

These things must be checked prior to starting an attack, and after a long drawn out engagement, they should be rechecked as you consider your escape options. If your batteries are low during an attack and you plan a submerged escape, it would be a good idea to start conserving your battery charge by reducing your submerged speed. Also, it might be wise to shoot from a little further out than normal to allow extra time to submerge to a safe depth, rig for silent running, and wait it out.

If you forget to keep an eye on your oxygen level, you are in for serious trouble. If this is the case, and you realize it before you are committed, make the wise move and withdraw temporarily to charge your batteries and restore your oxygen level.

Know Where the Bottom Is

This is important for two reasons. First, you do not want to find it unexpectedly and beach your command, and second, you can use it to your advantage by settling down on it and quietly letting the escorts lose track of you. In shallow water and in deep dives, you want to pay extra attention to the bottom. A beached sub is as good as dead.

Consider Your Damage Level

Obviously, damage that reduces your ability to dive or surface will be considered as you make decisions, but there are other types of damage which can be equally important in planning your evasion tactics. When scanning your damage report, keep alert for reports of leaking fuel or dropping air pressure. These leaks will appear on the surface and point a finger directly at you and make it almost impossible to shake an enemy destroyer. When confronted with this situation, your choices are limited to going deep and waiting it out or trying the next tactic.

Debris Decoy

Most of the simulations have a debris-decoy feature which can be used only once during a war patrol. This tactic was used far more frequently in the movies than in real life, but it can give you a second chance when all else fails.

Hiding Under the Bed

Another when-all-else-fails tactic is to run toward the ships and hide under them as you go deeper (rather than running away from the convoy while trying to get deeper). This is often difficult, but it can be a lifesaver in some situations.

CHAPTER 7

Tips and Hints
for Playing
Silent Service

7
Tips and Hints
for Playing
Silent Service

Silent Service is manufactured and distributed by:
MicroProse
120 Lake Front Dr.
Hunt Valley, MD 21030
(301) 667-1151

Silent Service has been around for a number of years, but it remains one of the best simulation games of any kind. The main objective of this game is to beat the U.S.S *Tang*'s single patrol record of 39,300 tons of shipping sunk. Maybe some of the following ideas and tips will help you achieve this difficult mission.

Practice
If you're just starting out with *Silent Service,* it is well worth the time to use the Torpedo/Gun Practice scenario to get a basic feel for all of the weapons you will be using in combat. Be sure to practice using the deck gun as it takes some time to learn to use it properly, and you may not have any time to practice once out on patrol.

Skill Levels
At the start of the game, you will be asked to choose a skill level. The level that you choose will have a lot to do with how difficult the game will be. The skill level affects a number of things, but the two most important are the amount of damage caused by enemy depth charges and the amount of damage you need to inflict in order to sink an enemy ship.

As the skill levels go up, you can be damaged more severely by depth charges which also need not be as close as in easier levels. The combination of torpedo hits and deck-gun hits required to sink a ship also goes up with the levels. Midshipman, Lieutenant, and Commander levels all require two torpedo hits to sink a ship; however, one torpedo hit can be followed up with deck-gun fire. The amount of deck-gun fire necessary to cause the ship to sink increases with the level. At the Captain level, three torpedo hits or a lot of deck-gun fire are required.

Reality Levels

Choosing the correct reality levels and knowing how they impact the game will have a major effect on how well you do and how much you enjoy the simulation.

Limited Visibility. This factor will affect how enemy ships are handled on your chart screens. If you select this factor, you will only have information regarding enemy ship positions that would actually be available. If the ships are not close in sight (either through the periscope or from the surface indicator), dots on the chart will blink at the ship's last known position. If you are traveling submerged at periscope depth, you can update your information on the chart screen by popping the periscope up and quickly putting it back down; it is not necessary to go to the periscope screen and actually look through it. If this factor is not chosen, the enemy ships will always appear on the chart.

Convoy Zigzags. If this level is selected, the convoys will zigzag as they head toward their destination. It should be noted that these course changes are regular, so by observing the convoy for a short period you can determine how much time passes between course changes. This information is very important in your attack execution: If your target changes course while your torpedoes are on the way, they will likely miss. It is a good idea to fire as soon after a zig as possible.

Dud Torpedoes. As explained in the operator's manual, the Allies had a number of torpedo troubles during the early part of the war. If you choose this reality factor and choose a sub in the early part of the war, be prepared to suffer some of

All quiet on the surface as lookouts keep watch through the surface haze for targets.

the same frustration felt by actual sub commanders as they watched perfect setups disappear in the splash of a dud torpedo.

Port Repairs Only. Once you begin to gain confidence in your abilities to evade enemy escorts, you may choose to add this factor to improve your scores. Using this factor requires you to use much more care during your approach and attack, because if you are spotted and receive a good going over by depth charges, anything that gets broken will remain broken. However, if you have successfully completed a number of patrols with no damage, you might want to try this factor. It will definitely add excitement to the game.

Expert Destroyers. The designers mean what they say here. If this factor is chosen, the enemy escorts are much better, so be prepared. They will spot you much farther away, so make your end-arounds a little wider. They are also very tenacious in their attack once they have you spotted. You won't be able to just go deep and wait for them to go away; they will hang around forever. To get away, you must move below a thermal level and move away at very slow speed, keeping a minimum profile (if these tactics are possible).

Convoy Search. After you come off the big chart back to realtime, if you choose this level, the position of the convoy might not appear on the chart. If this is the case, you can locate the convoy position by looking through the periscope or binoculars. To get the ships to appear on the map, you will need to move closer, until they change from dots on the horizon to identifiable vessels. They will always appear, no matter how distant, if this factor is not selected.

Angle-on-the-Bow Input. Inputting the angle-on-the-bow data is the most difficult of the reality factors. It was also difficult for the actual sub commanders, and they had actual ships to look at. Judging this angle from looking at the graphic shapes of the ships is almost impossible. There are, however, a couple of other ways to go about using this factor.

Preset the situation at the firing point and then maneuver to meet these preset conditions. In other words, decide beforehand on an angle that is easy to determine, such as 90 degrees. At 90 degrees of angle-on-the-bow, the enemy ship would be totally broadside to you. To do this follow these steps:

1. Determine the target heading.
2. Obtain a position ahead of the target, close to the target track.
3. Stop and take a heading perpendicular to the target track. (For example, if the target heading is 270 degrees, your heading would be either 180 degrees or 0 degrees. Take the target track and subtract or add 90 to get the proper heading.)
4. Set the angle-on-the-bow in the Torpedo Data Computer to +90 or −90 degrees. If the target is moving across your bow from right to left, use the −90 setting. If it is moving from left to right, use the +90 setting.
5. Wait until the target is directly in front of you (target bearing and your heading are equal) and shoot.

The other method is to leave the angle at zero and shoot to lead the target. This is called using the *hosepipe* method, where you aim the sub as you would a gun. Remember the more distant the target or the faster it is moving the more you need to lead it. Also, larger angles require more lead, narrow angles need less lead, and ships heading directly toward or away from you require no lead angle at all.

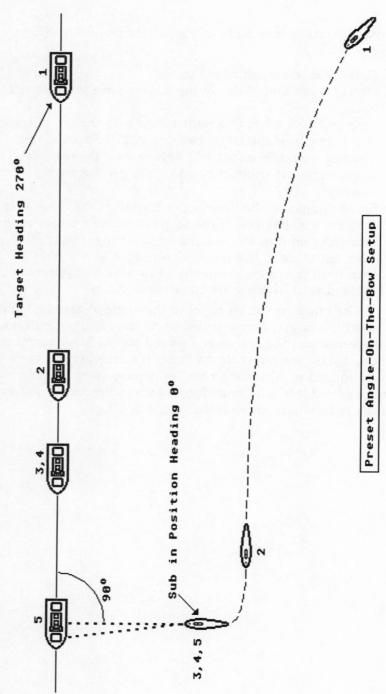

Target Heading 270°

Sub in Position Heading 0°

90°

Preset Angle-On-The-Bow Setup

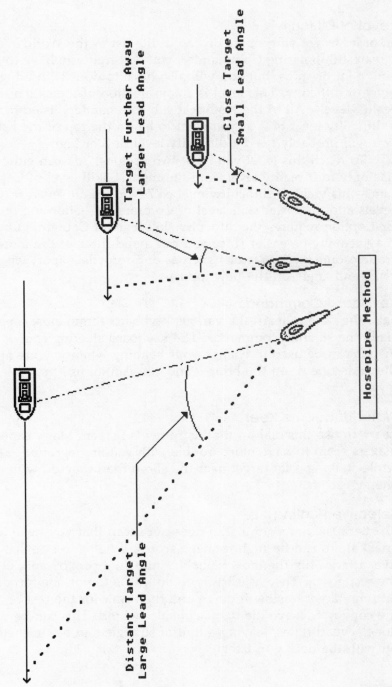

Target Further Away
Larger Lead Angle

Close Target
Small Lead Angle

Hosepipe Method

Distant Target
Large Lead Angle

Level of Difficulty

In order to get your name on top of the list as the World's Greatest Submarine Commander, you will not only have to sink a lot of ships, but you will also have to do it with a high level of difficulty. This level is a combination of the skill and reality levels. All of the historical sub commanders listed have a difficulty level of 7. If you want to be on the top of the list you will probably need a difficulty level of 7 or higher.

To reach this level you have two options. You can either use only four reality levels and the highest skill level of Captain—this yields a difficulty level of 7—or use all seven reality levels and the lower skill level of Commander. Choosing the first option requires the difficulty skill level of Captain, but may actually be easier since you can avoid three of the more troublesome reality factors (such as dud torpedoes, port repairs only, and angle-on-the-bow input).

Keyboard Commands

Take the time to learn the various keyboard commands, especially the steering commands. The keyboard steering commands can be used to change your heading when you are at the periscope or on the bridge, and you cannot use the joystick.

Water Under the Keel

Learn to use this dial on the Instruments Screen. Many expert players seem to have more trouble with running aground while stalking a fat target near the shore than they do with enemy escorts.

Selective Hunting

Just because you sight a ship does not mean that you have to attack it. To run up high tonnage scores, it helps to be selective; attack only the most valuable ships in a convoy and let the rest go on. The easiest way to do this is to put one torpedo into the target to slow it down and then wait for the rest of the convoy to leave the damaged ship behind. This can be done several times, leaving a trail of stragglers to be finished off with the deck gun later.

Note the Base Course

Make a mental note of the convoy base course before you start your attack as the ships will scatter and change course once your presence has been detected. After a few minutes, if you have not been sighted or located by the escorts, the convoy will normally return to its previous course. Keeping this in mind, you can attack quickly and retreat on a course which will put you in a favorable position once the convoy resumes its previous heading.

Maneuvering in Advanced Time Scale

When in the fast time mode, you can change your heading, and the ship will turn as though you were in normal time. This will help you steer in this mode, but can be a disadvantage because the escorts will be maneuvering in fast time and will be able to outmaneuver you. So, if you are trying to evade the enemy, go back to normal time where you have the maneuvering advantage.

Changing depth, however, is different. If you are in fast time mode and give the dive command, the sub will dive very quickly, so quickly, in fact, that you may go below the test depth before you know it. Surfacing in fast time mode poses a similar danger as you could wind up on the surface next to a destroyer unexpectedly. Diving while in fast time mode when being attacked does seem to get you deep faster, but you need to keep an eye on your depth.

Safe Depth

Recall that the Japanese were not aware of the depth capabilities of our subs and consequently set their depth charges to explode at too shallow a depth. If you can get to a depth of 200 feet, or more, you will be safe from depth-charge attacks. The enemy will still be able to find you at that depth, so to get cleanly away, you may need to go deeper to find a temperature layer. Once at that depth, you will be very hard to detect and can move about with less chance of being detected. Expert destroyers might still be able to hear you when directly over you, so if you are trying to evade expert-level destroyers, do so at very slow speeds and stop engines when they pass over you.

Time-Period Advantages

The time periods available each have their advantages and disadvantages. If you choose to operate early in the war, you have a better chance of encountering unescorted convoys, but you will have to use old steam-powered torpedoes which leave a trail pointing back to your position. If there are escorts, they will know the exact location from which you attacked.

If you operate late in the war, all of the convoys will be escorted, but you will be equipped with electric torpedoes which leave no trail. Therefore, you can make repeated attacks from the same position without being detected. Also, the later subs had a greater maximum-depth capability which allowed them to find deeper temperature layers.

Save Deck-Gun Ammo

Use your deck gun sparingly. Do not waste your shots. Nothing is more frustrating than having a damaged ship stopped dead in the water with your last torpedo shot and finding out that you are also out of deck-gun ammunition. In this situation, ramming the ship is not an option. This will only result in the loss of your sub and a lower final rank.

Docked Ships

Occasionally, when searching near the shore, you will find a ship stopped and docked. Approach these ships very carefully. Many subs end up beached trying to attack docked ships. Also, be aware that if the chart shows land between you and the ship, the land still might not appear through the periscope or from the bridge view. Generally it is best to trust the chart in these cases. You can find out for sure by firing a torpedo, if it explodes before it gets to the ship, then you know that there is land between you and the target. By doing this, though, you run the risk of alerting the enemy to your presence.

Slowing Targets

Once you have been detected, the ships in the convoy will speed up to ten knots, making it almost impossible to gain a good firing position while submerged. If you have an unescorted convoy running from you, it will be necessary to surface to catch them. Once you get close to them, you can slow them down by putting a couple of deck-gun rounds into them. When you've got them going only five knots or so, you can submerge to gain a position on their flank and will have a broad torpedo target.

CHAPTER 8

Tips and Hints for Playing
GATO

8
Tips and Hints
for Playing
GATO

GATO is manufactured and distributed by:
Spectrum Holobyte
1050 Walnut St.
Suite 325
Boulder, CO 80302
(303) 443-0191

GATO was one of the first submarine simulation games and
has been around for several years. This game has been period-
ically updated, so if you have owned *GATO* for a number of
years, you might want to check with the manufacturer to see if
an updated version exists. The most recent Commodore 64
version is 1.0. Here are a few hints and ideas which should
help you improve your chances for mission success.

Before Your Next Mission
Once you have successfully completed the first mission, there
is one thing you can do to increase your chance of success on
the next mission. You should go to the Change Parameters
screen and move to a safe corner of the patrol area. I use coordinates 1000,1000, but any corner except the northeast corner will do. This will allow you to start the next mission in a
safe area. Nothing is more frustrating than starting a new mission, appearing in the middle of a convoy, and being destroyed with no chance to react. This will also give you a
chance to surface, recharge your batteries, and replenish your
oxygen level.

Down-the-Throat

Very rarely will you have the opportunity to hit a destroyer with a broadside shot. They will normally be heading toward you and must be destroyed with a down-the-throat shot. This is best accomplished while you are submerged and using reverse power. The following example shows one of the best ways to deal with the typical three-ship convoy which you will encounter.

1. You have the convoy in sight and are heading for it on the surface.
2. The escorts spot you and start pinging with sonar. You should immediately submerge to periscope depth (which will make your speed drop to zero) and apply reverse power (buying time to shoot at the escorts and give you the speed you need to maneuver and line up your targets).
3. Once the first escort starts to get larger fire two torpedoes, lower the scope, and start going deep (a precautionary measure in case you miss). When you hear an explosion check the radar to make sure the first escort has disappeared.
4. Repeat the above procedure with the second escort.
5. When the escorts have been taken care of, surface and apply full power to chase the transport.
6. Once you have the transport in range, slow down and fire one-shot salvos until you sink it.

   Do not get too close to the transports. Care should be taken when approaching a transport as there are no visual clues to tell you that you are about to collide. The ship will appear the same size at 1000 yards or 100 yards, so approach slowly and check the range readout often. If you approach to less than 200 yards or so, you will be destroyed.

Ships Close to and Behind Islands

In order to sink a ship close to an island, you will have to draw it out. Sand bars and reefs will prevent your torpedoes from getting to the enemy ship unless you fire from just the right angle. Ships which are behind an island can track you on sonar, so you will hear the pings, but they cannot go through the island to attack you. Keep an eye on them, but they are usually not a threat.

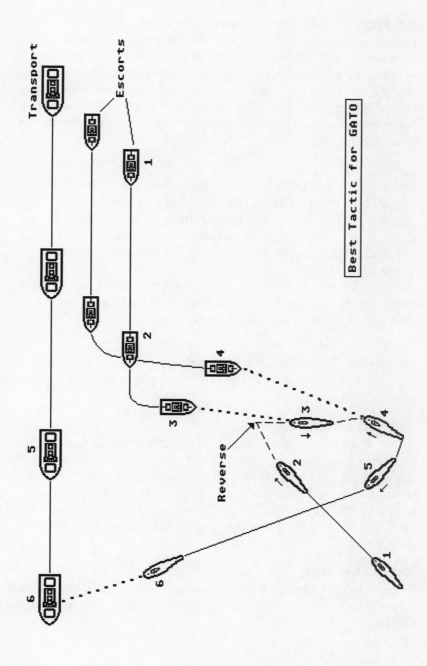

The Edge of the Patrol Area

Convoys which are approaching the edge of the patrol area
are just as well left alone unless you just want to sink some
destroyers. You can chase after these convoys, but chances are
that by the time you finish dealing with the escorts the transport ship will disappear. It's infuriating to have a transport all
lined up, shoot a couple of torpedoes at it, and then watch it
disappear as it goes out of the patrol area.

Back to the Base

The coordinates 1450,8600 will put you back at the base for
repairs and torpedo refill. The number of torpedoes on board
will not update until you change the screen, but they are
there. If you are damaged and cannot get away from the enemy to change coordinates, you can ask for a new mission.
Make sure that the new mission you accept starts the enemy
out in a distant location or you will be right back in the same
mess. Once the new mission starts, you can change your coordinates and get back to the base.

The Mainland

Frequently, your mission orders will mention the mainland,
but will not tell you where that is. It appears that the mainland is to the east.

Difficulty Levels

There does not appear to be a lot of difference in the various
difficulty levels except that levels 4 and 5 do not show the
convoys on the chart. It is a good idea to play a number of
missions in the lower difficulty levels. There are very few missions, so once you have played them all, you will have a good
idea of where to find the convoys in the higher difficulty
levels.

Turning the Sub

Your speed affects the turning rate of the sub, so if you are in
a hurry to turn around to use your stern tubes, crank up the
speed.

Periscope view of torpedo hitting distant Japanese ship.

Maximum Depth

You can go as deep as you like, but do not go deeper than the gauge reads. Do not go all the way around to the zero again or your sub will be destroyed with no warning.

Use the Radar

When operating in the lower difficulty levels, the radar is of little use as all the ships appear on the chart screen. Radar is helpful, however, during close-in fights with destroyers. When at levels 4 and 5, using the radar is the only way to locate enemy convoys beyond visual range. Whenever using these higher levels, always consult the radar when making decisions.

CHAPTER 9

Tips and Hints
for Playing
Up Periscope!

9
Tips and Hints
for Playing
Up Periscope!

Up Periscope! is distributed by:
ActionSoft
122-4 S. Race St.
Urbana, Il 64801
(217) 367-1024

I and a number of friends and acquaintances all across the country have spent many enjoyable hours playing and discussing *Up Periscope!*. Here are a number of particularly helpful tips and hints for increasing your scores and confidence as a sub commander.

Training
If you are just starting with the game, take the time to try the Refresher Training at New London. Going through this exercise will help familiarize you with the boat's control and weapons commands. Although the target ships are not moving, they will turn away from you (if you are spotted) to present the smallest target for you to shoot at. So approach deep and slow.

Using the Chart
You need to be aware that the ships indicated on the Chart Display only give you an approximate indication of their direction of travel. They may appear to be traveling on a heading of 130 degrees when they are actually on a heading of 150 degrees. Use the Torpedo Data Computer to establish their true course. Take this reading off of one of the cargo ships in the convoy, not one of the escorts. They may zigzag somewhat.

War Patrols

Using the historical situations provided can be fun for short games or to demonstrate the software to a friend, but for the real excitement of commanding a sub and advancing in rank, go to the War Patrol section. Using this section of the software will present you with many different situations and help keep the game fresh and enjoyable.

Save Your Game to Disk

It will become obvious to you after a couple of games that you cannot jump from Lieutenant to Admiral in one session, so to pick up where you left off later use the SAVE GAME option on the End Game menu. Don't use your game disk: It will be erased.

You should also use the SAVE GAME option after a successful encounter to make sure you can start from this point if you sink during your next encounter. Also, if you are going to try something new or dangerous, save your current standing just in case it does not work out. This feature of the game allows you to be adventuresome and daring without having to worry about having to start over with no ships sunk.

Speed Changes

Be aware that your speed changes in an analog—as opposed to a digital—fashion. In other words, ordering flank speed from a standstill will not immediately give a speed of 20 knots; the speed will slowly build up to 20 knots. Follow this advice when slowing down, too. Stopping the engines will not immediately stop the boat, you will coast for a distance. If you need to stop in a hurry, you can apply reverse engines. If you're on the surface, submerging will also slow you down a lot. Keep this in mind when operating in shallow waters as you can easily coast up onto the shore and beach your sub.

Operating in Reverse

When using reverse speed, all controls will operate in the opposite fashion. This may seem fairly obvious, but it also applies to the diving controls. Ordering a dive while in reverse will cause the sub to surface and vice versa. This can be a

Captain lines up a target with the TBT, Target Bearing Transmitter.

good thing to know if your diving planes get damaged and you cannot surface. If you should find yourself with your diving planes stuck in the down position and your boat is heading past its maximum depth, you do not have to use the emergency surface function. Simply apply reverse power and you should be able to maintain your depth until the damage can be repaired.

Dangers of the Advanced Time Scale

Using the advanced time scale to speed things up is a great help, but care should be taken while using this function. It is not advisable to try to turn the boat or change depth while in fast time. This fast time scale makes everything move faster, so if you apply full left rudder to make a minor course change, you will wind up spinning rapidly in circles before you know it. The same thing applies to changing your depth while in fast time. Trying to do this could pop you up on the surface in plain view of the convoy or immediately put you down to 900 feet.

Also, making an approach in fast speed can be dangerous; if you are sighted, a destroyer will be on you in no time, at 32 times normal speed.

Keep Your Computer Cool

This type of game requires that you keep your computer on for extended periods of time; doing so can cause it to get hot and lock up. If this happens, there is nothing you can do but turn the computer off and reboot the software. That is why it is a good idea to save your game to disk often during long sessions. Nothing is more frustrating after having sunk ten ships than watching helplessly while the software locks up and you lose it all.

Water Temp Dial

Locate and use the water temp dial. This will tell you when you pass beneath a temperature gradient or layer. Once this occurs the enemy will have great difficulty in tracking you. Making your approach under a layer will allow you to get much closer without being sighted.

Set Periscope Direction

A beneficial feature of this software is that it allows you to align the direction of the periscope prior to raising it. Anytime you are going to raise the scope, look at the chart first to determine the approximate direction of the target and point the scope in that direction before you put it up. This will greatly decrease the amount of time that the scope is visible and decrease your chance of being spotted.

Using the Big Chart

The first time I played this game, I selected the War Patrol feature, picked a sub and the north Pacific area, and spent the next half-hour wandering around without making a single contact with the enemy. It took me awhile to figure out that I was in the wrong territory. The following chart should help you avoid making the same mistake.

#	Submarine	Patrol Area
1	USS *Wahoo*, Second Patrol	North Pacific
2	USS *Wahoo*, Sixth Patrol	North Pacific
3	USS *Tang*, First Patrol	South Pacific
4	USS *Tang*, Third Patrol	South Pacific
5	USS *Tang*, Sixth Patrol	North Pacific
6	USS *Guardfish*, First Patrol	North Pacific
7	USS *Harder*, Second Patrol	North Pacific

The big chart can also be used for a number of creative purposes.

1. If you are in serious trouble and about to be sunk or destroyed, you can zip to the big chart and escape.
2. If you need to reload torpedoes during an encounter, you can go to the big chart, go to the next area, apply full rudder, and increase the time scale to the maximum. Doing this will cause you to sail around in circles and load your torpedoes quickly. Once you are loaded, go back to the big chart and return to the area where you last saw the convoy.
3. A successful attack often leaves you damaged and low on battery power and oxygen. If you head straight for another convoy, by using the big chart, you will arrive in the same condition. If you find yourself in this situation, use the big

chart to go to an unoccupied area and travel on the surface in the fast time scale to recharge the batteries, repair damage, and replenish your oxygen. Now you are ready to attack another convoy in top condition.

Avoid Destroyers Traveling Alone

Often when moving around on the big chart, you will encounter a single destroyer traveling alone, or you may have sunk an entire convoy leaving only the escort afloat. In these circumstances, it is best to move on and not attack. It is very difficult to successfully complete this kind of attack, and you are better off saving your torpedoes to fry larger fish.

Identify All Convoy Ships First

Before you start shooting, it is best to identify all the ships using the TDC. By doing this, you will establish the position of the escorts. If there are no escorts, you can use a much more aggressive attack tactic. If escorts are present, then you will know the relative values of all the ships and be able to choose the most valuable ship for an extra torpedo or two.

Using the Manual TDC

Using the TDC in the manual mode is not difficult, is closer to the real thing in terms of simulation realism, and will improve your score due to the increased difficulty. Follow these steps and you should have little difficulty.

1. Follow the directions of the sequencer line. When it says *Take a mark*, align the periscope on the middle of the target and press the MARK button for your particular computer. After doing this, it should say *Take another mark*. It is very important that you wait at least 50 seconds before taking your second mark. You can take a mark before this time, and the TDC will indicate that it is locked on the target, but your chance of a hit is slim, so use some patience and wait close to a minute.
2. If time permits, and as you reach the higher ranks, it is best to take a third mark.
3. If you are very close to the target track, remember to take your first mark early because the target will move very

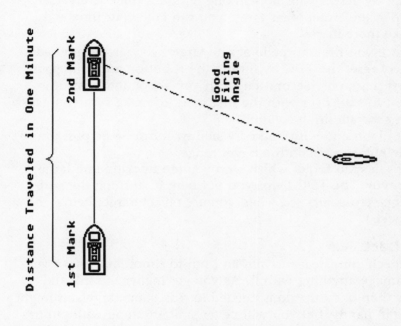

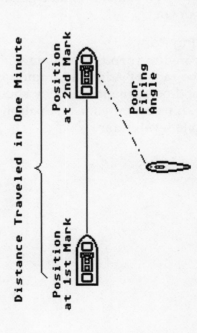

quickly across your bow in one minute's time. Conversely when the target is far away, you can take your time and take more marks.

4. Once you fire a torpedo at one target, you should immediately reset the TDC by hitting the R button and take your first mark on a second target. If you shoot and miss, it is best to start over with the first mark to make sure you get an accurate firing solution.
5. At night, and with limited visibility, it can be helpful to use the radar to obtain the target range.
6. It is easy to forget which ship you are tracking in a large convoy. The TDC helps you out here by turning the periscope crosshairs red when you are on the target being tracked.

The Deck Gun

The deck gun is easy to aim and fun to shoot, but I have yet to damage anything with it. As you get higher in rank and more than one torpedo is needed to sink some targets, it might come in handy, but you will never sink anything with gunfire only. I put 70 rounds into a cargo ship, and it never even slowed down.

Acquiring Rank

Be prepared to spend some time with this game if you want to reach the rank of Admiral. Promotions come slowly and only with good performance, as they should. You may sink 200,000 tons of shipping on your first patrol, but you will only advance one level in rank.

Best-Bet Tactic

Using the following tactic should put quite a few Japanese
ships on the bottom:

1. You have a convoy sighted and are approaching on the surface. You want to be spotted by the enemy, but at a great
   distance.
2. The escort ship spots you and heads in your direction. As
   soon as you are sighted, dive to 100 feet and head away
   from the escort.
3. Due to your quick reaction, the escort ship cannot locate
   you and begins to circle trying to find you. You keep heading for the convoy.
4. The escort gives up and resumes its previous course but
   does not go back to the convoy. You have a great position
   between the convoy and the escort. Go to periscope depth
   and shoot.

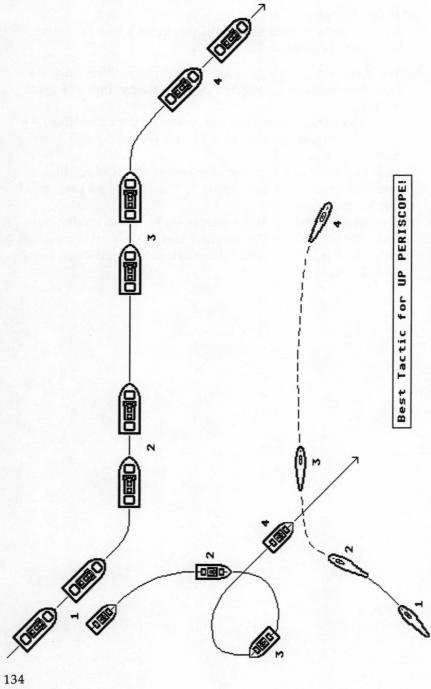

Best Tactic for UP PERISCOPE!

CHAPTER 10

Tips and Hints for Playing
Sub Battle Simulator

10
Tips and Hints
for Playing
Sub Battle Simulator

Sub Battle Simulator is distributed by:
Epyx
600 Galveston Dr.
P.O. Box 8020
Redwood City, CA 94063
(415) 366-0606

The latest entry into the submarine simulation arena is *Sub Battle* from Epyx of Redwood City, California. It is obvious that the designers of this game tried to do more than just make a clone of *Silent Service*. They have created an original, though sometimes frustrating, game. The following tips and hints should help get you past the initial frustration and on to enjoying this exciting simulation.

Training Mission
The training mission provided with this simulation is more than just shooting fish in a barrel. You are given a large moving convoy to attack and escorts which will shoot back and attempt to ram you, so use caution when approaching this training convoy; you don't want to lose your command in a training exercise.

Note Your Boat
Upon receiving your orders make note of the type of boat you are going to be commanding during your mission. Both German and American scenarios offer two very different subs. You will need to adjust your tactics if you go to sea in a U.S.

S-boat or a German Type II. These subs were slower, could not dive as deep, carried few torpedoes, and most did not have aft torpedo tubes.

Keep Your Provisions in Mind

When leaving on a long-distance patrol, it is best to maximize the use of your food and fuel by choosing a fast travel speed. You do not have to use the speed which is recommended by the computer. Also, when on station on long-distance patrols, it is best to conserve fuel. So don't go dashing off across the ocean chasing a convoy that you cannot catch. You might not be able to get back home.

Keep Those Batteries Charged

One of the most common mistakes players make with this game is forgetting to switch back to diesel engines and putting the batteries back on charge once you surface. Leaving the electric motors on and going to a fast time scale will cause your batteries to go dead in no time at all. It is possible with this simulation, unlike others, to charge the batteries while sitting still on the surface.

Do Not Panic When Sighting Smoke

The first reaction most players have when seeing smoke on the horizon is to dive. Doing this not only makes your approach take much longer (if you can catch the enemy ships at all), but also leaves you with depleted batteries when you are ready to attack. When smoke is sighted, it is best to continue on the surface until just before the ships appear on the 35-mile screen or until you get the Battle Stations signal. The optimum condition is to dive just prior to the Battle Stations command.

Go to the Tower for Planes

When you are being attacked by planes, it is best to go to the tower view. The other views are too restricted vertically to allow you maintain contact with the plane once it gets close. If you need to use the scope during this situation, remove the 7× function.

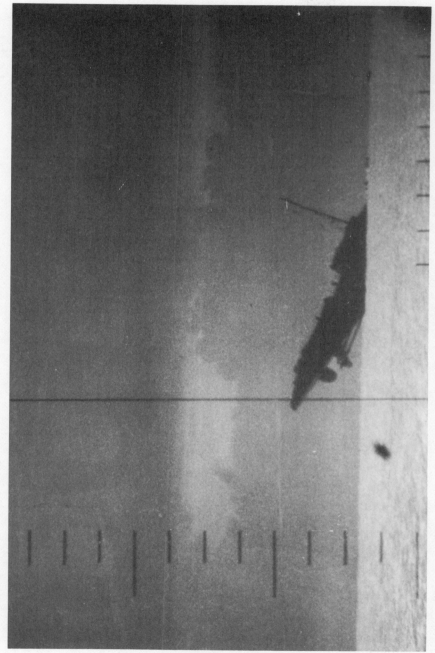

Fatally torpedoed by the USS *Seawolf*, Japanese patrol boat Number 39 sinks by the bow. Photo taken through periscope.

Stay On Station

It is very easy when chasing a convoy to wander off of your assigned station. This is okay, but time spent off station does not count toward your days-on-station rating. If you are not sure of your position, or if midnight passes and you do not get a days-on-station update, then you are out of position. In this case, check your orders for the proper coordinates and then check your current position. If you are uncertain about which direction will get you back to the correct coordinates, then go to the Status Screen and start to move. Note how your position changes and adjust your heading until the numbers are changing in the right direction. You will receive a message when you reenter the patrol area.

Saving Your Game

Although the manual states that you need a formatted disk on which to save your current game, this is not correct. Don't use a separate disk, use your game disk. This means that you can only have one game at a time saved. It is a good idea to use this feature often. Every time you have a good encounter, save your game. That way if you get killed later, you can start back and keep credit for your most recent sinkings.

Hall of Fame

While in my first series of Wartime Command missions, I spent a lot of time trying to figure out how to update the Hall of Fame with my latest accomplishments. I later found out that this screen will only update when you are killed, when you lose your command (if you get a zero-percent rating you will lose your command), or if you live through the entire war.

Dealing with Destroyers

It seems that no matter what you try, once an escort or a destroyer knows that you are out there, they will not go away and you cannot get away from them. Keep this in mind. One tactic that seems to work well is to pick two large targets out of the convoy and shoot one torpedo at each, one hit will not sink them, but it will slow them down enough so that once you have dealt with the escorts, you can catch up and finish them off.

Now that you have hit the convoy, all the escort ships will head toward you. The general plan here is to sink them in order with down-the-throat torpedo shots as they come at you. Shoot two torpedoes at the closest attacker and then two more at the next one if you are in a sub with six forward tubes. Now swing the sub around, shoot at the next closest target with the aft tubes, and increase speed to the max in order to buy some time for a reload. If the bad guys get close and start dropping depth charges, your best bet is to try to stay out from under them until they run out of charges. Once they are out of charges you can pop up to periscope depth, fire a couple of torpedoes, and sink back down again to avoid being rammed. (Remember, you can be rammed at periscope depth.) If you have the escort lined up, you don't even have to risk putting the periscope up to aim. Repeat this procedure until they are all on the bottom or you are out of torpedoes; if this happens, your only hope is to surface and try to get them with the deck gun.

Using the Deck Gun
The deck guns provided have different ranges depending on the type of sub you are assigned, so make a note of the deck-gun range for your sub when you set out on patrol. These guns are generally very accurate in this simulation, but be aware that the enemy surface ships have larger guns with longer range. So stay submerged until you are within your range if you must use the deck gun against an armed ship.

Mines
Occasionally you will receive orders to lay mines while on station. Once these mines are laid, stay away from them; they will explode and damage your sub if you get close to them. Do not try to go under them either. I was once damaged by a mine, which I laid on the surface, when I came back to that area at 200 feet. I have also tried to use these mines as offensive or defensive weapons; that is, laying these mines in the path of a convoy or dropping them behind me as a destroyer was closing in. I have had no success with this tactic. The only ship to hit one of these mines has been my sub.

Torpedo Operation

The torpedoes of this game require you to lead the target in order to gain a hit. Doing this requires a good bit of practice as you must take into account the target direction, target speed, and target distance. Down-the-throat and up-the-kilt shots are useful as no lead is required.

Time Scales

The time scale feature can be both useful and frustrating. When waiting on station in the 1–10 minute mode it can take forever for anything to happen. However if you speed up to 1–4 hour mode, things can happen so quickly that convoys pass you by before you have time to react. The only advice that I can offer is that the latter seems to occur in the German command more than in the American command. This is possibly due to the short distances many convoys travel in European waters. It is best to wait in the 1–10 minute mode when in the confined space of European coastal waters and the English Channel.

Performance Review

Pay attention to your orders. If your orders say spend 20 days on station, then stay 20 days or you will receive a poor review. These reviews do not mean a lot since there is no promotion ladder to be climbed. You can, however, lose your command as a result of an extremely bad performance.

Depth Ratings

The side-view screen displays the maximum rated depth for that sub. This depth, however, seems to have little to do with the readings on the depth gauge. Subs rated to 900 feet will crush at about 600 feet on the gauge, subs rated to 750 feet will crush somewhat sooner. Your best bet is to dive until you get a *We are too deep* message and then go a little bit deeper, but don't push it. Remember, you cannot trust the gauge.

CHAPTER 11

In the Captain's Own Words

11
In the Captain's Own Words

Finally, to get a real feel for what it was like to actually be involved in submarine warfare, here are excerpts from several sub commander's reports to their superiors. Each of the attacks described illustrate one of the tactics previously discussed.

Commander Richard H. O'kane

Commander Richard H. O'kane was arguably the best sub commander of the war. From his very first patrol aboard the U.S.S *Tang*, he and his crew experienced amazing success. On the morning of February 25, 1944 the *Tang* attacked a convoy using a parallel approach tactic. Commander O'kane described the action as follows:

February 25, 1944
Attack #5
0548
At 0548, with skies grey in the east, submerged to radar depth, took a last check at range 7000 yards, then started a submerged approach to close an apparent 30-degree left zig. Eighteen minutes later the tanker was in sight with an ASASHIO-type destroyer patrolling very close ahead. As we were then 1200 yards from the track, turned and paralleled his base course. At range 2000 yards, the destroyer gave us some bad moments by crossing to our bow for the second time, pointing directly at our position. But in his attempt to avoid a repetition of his mistake the night before, he turned right, passed down the tanker's starboard side to that quarter.

He was absolutely dwarfed by the length of the loaded tanker, whose details were now plainly visible. She was painted slate grey, comparable only to our CIMARRON class, but with bridge and foremast well forward, just behind a bulging bow, which mounted an estimated six-inch gun. Her mainmast was close against her after superstructure which was stopped by an extremely large short stack. Her after gun, above her bulging cruiser stern, was similar to the one forward. There is no similar vessel in any of the identification books aboard. All vantage points including guns, bridge, bridge overhead, and rails were manned with an estimated 150 uniformed lookouts on our side alone.

A 20-degree zig toward put us a little close to the track, but as we had already commenced our turn away for a stern shot, we were far from inconvenienced. At 0639, with the escort just crossing the tanker's stern to the far side, fired four torpedoes by constant bearings, range 500 yards, 90 starboard track, gyros around 180 degrees. The first three hit as aimed, directly under the stack, at the forward end of his after superstructure, and under his bridge. The explosions were wonderful, throwing . . . debris above the belching smoke. He sank by the stern in four minutes, and then we went deep and avoided. The depth charges started a minute later, but were never close.

During his fourth war patrol, Commander O'kane was lucky enough to come across a ship at anchor. Even with this advantage, he still faced some tight moments as he experienced a number of torpedo problems.

August 22, 1944
Attack #6
0020
After passing MIKI SAKI, slowed, crossed the 100-fathom curve and proceeded around KUKI SAKI into OWASE WAN. We soon found "a pip where no pip ought to be." The night was black and only the long shape of the enemy could be seen until we circled him to get away from the land background. There he was quite visible, identified as the gunboat who had harassed us during our first visit, topping it off with those tooth-shakers. He tracked at zero speed and was obviously anchored in about 20 fathoms two miles northwest of KUKI SAKI.

Commander Richard O'kane at the periscope aboard the USS *Tang*.

0142
Holding our breath, we moved in slowly to twelve-hundred
yards, twisted, then steadied for a straight stern shot and fired
one Mark 18-1 torpedo at his middle set on three feet. The
phosphorescent wake petered out after a hundred-yard run
with the torpedo evidently heading down, and hit bottom
with a loud rumble, timed half way to the enemy, where there
should have been 250 feet of water. It was tracked by sound
to this moment, but after the rumble cleared away, nothing
more was heard.

0144
Fired a second Mark 18-1 torpedo set on three feet feeling
sure the enemy had been alerted by the first. Its wake was
dimly visible directly to the target, tracked also by sound, but
passed underneath, apparently running on the deep side, too.

0158
With one salvo of three left aft, circled for a bow shot, and
with range 900, fired a Mark 23 torpedo from number 5 tube
at his middle, set on zero feet. Though we were stopped and
absolutely steady and the gyro angle zero, it took a 30-yard
jog to the left before settling towards the target and missed
astern.

0200
Still whispering, though the last two torpedoes must have
roared past him, fired a second Mark 23 torpedo from number
six tube set on zero aimed at his gun forward. It took a jog to
the left also, but settled down right for his middle.

The explosion 40 seconds later was the most spectacular
we've ever seen, topped by a pillar of fire and more explosions about 500 feet in the air. There was absolutely nothing
left of the gunboat.

This vessel was observed at close hand previously during
daylight. She was new in appearance, flush deck, with raised
gun platforms forward and amidships mounting estimated
three-inch double-purpose guns. Aft of the midship platform
was a goal-post structure, possibly used for sweeping, topped
by a lookout or director platform. Her stern had very long

almost-horizontal depth-charge racks holding 14 counted depth charges a side, and what appeared to be Y-guns on the centerline. On observation before firing, she measured between 225 and 250 feet in length and is estimated to have a standard displacement of 1500 tons.

Feeling that our difficulties had been mainly in sluggish steering and depth engines, withdrew at full power to spend the day checking afterbodies of our remaining torpedoes.

The *Tang* conducted her fifth war patrol in the Formosa Straight. Once again the captain and crew performed in a commendable fashion. This is how Commander O'kane described one of their successful attack and escape encounters.

23 October, 1944
0030
On the first trial of the revamped SJ, the operator reported land at 11,000 yards where no land ought to be. Commenced tracking, immediately discovering a small pip moving out in our direction. Put him astern and bent on the screws. He evidently lost his original contact on us for he changed course and commenced a wide sweep about the convoy which was now also in sight. A submariner's dream quickly developed as we were able to assume the original position of this destroyer just ahead of the convoy while he went on a 20-mile inspection tour.

The convoy was composed of three large modern tankers in column, a transport on the starboard hand, a freighter on the port hand, flanked by DE's on both beams and quarters. After zigging with the convoy in position 3000 yards ahead, we dropped back between the tankers and the freighter. On the next zig, stopped and turned right for nearly straight bow shots at the tankers as they came by, firing two torpedoes under the stack and engine room space of the nearest tanker, a single torpedo into the protruding stern of the middle tanker, and two torpedoes under the stack and engine room space of the far tanker. The minimum range was 300 yards and the maximum 800 yards. Torpedoes were exploding before the firing was completed and all hit as aimed.

It was a terrific sight to see three blazing, sinking tankers, but there was only time for just a glance as the freighter was in position crossing our stern. Completed the set-up and was about to fire on this vessel when Leibold, my boatswain's mate, whom I've used for an extra set of eyes on all patrols, properly diagnosed the maneuvers of the starboard transport who was coming in like a destroyer attempting to ram. We were boxed in by the sinking tankers, the transport was too close for us to dive, so we had to cross his bow.

It was really a thriller-diller with the *Tang* barely getting on the inside of his turning circle and saving the stern with full left rudder in the last seconds. The transport commenced firing with large and small caliber stuff so cleared the bridge before realizing it was all above our heads. A quick glance aft, however showed the tables were again turned, for the transport was forced to continue her swing in an attempt to avoid colliding with the freighter which had also been coming to ram. The freighter struck the transport's starboard quarter shortly after we commenced firing four stern torpedoes spread along their double length. At a range of 400 yards, the crash coupled with the four torpedo explosions was terrific, sinking the freighter nose down almost instantly while the transport hung with a 30-degree up angle.

The destroyer was now coming in on our starboard quarter at 1300 yards with DE's on our port bow and beam. We headed for the DE on our bow so as to get the destroyer astern and greatfully watched the DE turn away, he apparently having seen enough. Our destroyer still hadn't lighted off another boiler and it was possible to open the range slowly, avoiding the last interested DE. When the radar range to the DD was 4500 yards, he gave up the chase and returned to the scene of the transport. We moved back, also as his bow still showed on the radar and its pip was visible. When we were 6000 yards off, however, another violent explosion took place and the bow disappeared both from sight and the radar screen. This explosion set off a gun duel amongst the destroyer and escort vessels who fired at random apparently sometimes at each other and sometimes just out into the night. Their confusion was truly complete. It looked like a good place to be away from so we cleared the area at full power until dawn.

Our attack log showed that only ten minutes had elapsed from the time of firing our first torpedo until that final explosion when the transport's bow went down.

Commander J. W. Coe

Another sub commander with the ability to improvise in a difficult situation was J. W. Coe, commander of the USS *Skipjack*. A miscalculation of the target track during a night attack led him to successfully complete the first down-the-throat sinking.

May 6, 1942
0300

At 0300, Z.D. −7, May 6, 1942 in Latitude 12-33 N., Longitude 109-30 E., own course 000 degrees, speed 5 knots, sighted vessel abeam to port, estimated range 15,000 yards, angle-on-the-bow 90 degrees port, on a southerly course. As we were between moon and target it appeared impossible to approach closer on surface undetected and accordingly own course was changed to 180 degrees and all engines put on at full speed in an effort to gain a position ahead before diving. *Skipjack* full speed turned out to be 16.4 knots due to foul bottom and high engine loads. This enabled us to draw ahead gradually, and at the same time we eased over to right in ten-degree increments as range increased. Maintained this speed until 0445 at which time we submerged, own course now being 240 degrees and target range about 18,000 yards with angle-on-the bow about 20 degrees port. Soon established target speed 11 knots, course 195 degrees, and we came to course 285 degrees for bow shots. I misgauged our approach speed in an effort to fire at low range and got in too close to wait for a favorable track and gyro angle. Let go when range was 650 yards and distance off track was about 300 with around 50 degrees right gyro angle indicated and 20 degree track. Fired three torpedoes with periscope and TDC solution, using as points of aim, 1- foremast, 2- amidships, 3- mainmast. A single load explosion occurred 34 seconds after firing first shot or 25 seconds after the firing of the second, and 14 seconds after firing third. Immediately after hearing explosion, raised periscope and observed target to be heeled badly to port, down by bow, and breaking into two just under stack amidships. Fuel was pouring out port side at the main deck evidently from full tanks. Her bow slid under, stern came out of water showing a big red single screw which never stopped turning over as she slipped down completely in just two minutes after being hit. The ship appeared to be heavily loaded, all deck spaces being filled with large boxes or crates, many of which floated clear as she went down. As sinking took place 6.5 miles east of Mui Rachtrang Light on Hon Lon Island (about 20 miles N.E. of Camranh Bay) in full view of lighthouse and other buildings on hills it was decided that discretion was the better part of valor and we crept off to the east at 150 feet fully expecting retaliatory measures which did not materialize. I got the impression of a gun aft but the target disappeared from view so fast while I attempted to size up various features of the vessel that this is not certain. She was quite large being about 6000 tons and about 450 feet in length. Although torpedo depth setting was ten feet it is believed that during 500–600 yard run, fish was not up to that depth and magnetic exploder took charge blowing entire bottom out of target and thus accounting for fast sinking. As I came to *Skipjack* just prior to this patrol and had become only slightly acquainted with the TDC since then, my intention on this first approach was to fire straight bow shots using the Mark VI angle solver for periscope bearing. I felt very sheepish in discovering I had overshot correct firing point with insufficient time and range for an adjustment. I was therefore profoundly impressed in discovering that ignoring my error in position, the TDC had kept grinding away and all was not yet lost; I give all credit to that magic box for the resultant hit and am now "convinced."

Commander D. C. White

Lieutenant Commander D. C. White commanded the USS *Plunger* with the ability to turn a bad situation into a successful sinking. One of these encounters was the first identified up-the-kilt sinking (angle-on-the-bow was 170 degrees) and was described as follows.

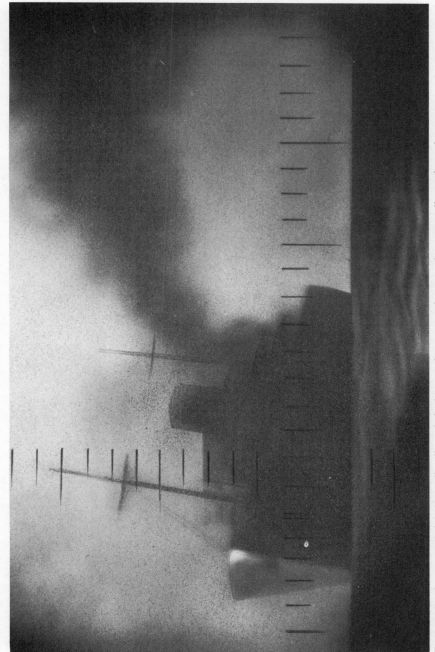

The result of a successful down-the-throat shot on a Japanese transport as seen through periscope.

June 30, 1942
0200
Sighted a large freighter bearing 350 degrees, distant 7 miles. Approximate position of freighter bearing 170 degrees, distant 3 miles from the Brothers Islands.

Freighter's approximate course 190 degrees. Commenced surface approach. Fired four bow tubes at ranges between 2500 and 1500 yards. Started firing at this range due to bright moonlight. Torpedoes missed. Made reload forward. Cut in all main generators and commenced chase at full power, 14.5 knots. Fired one bow tube at range of 400 yards, 170-degree track as ship was turning to starboard. Hit under after mast. The ship was probably loaded with explosives as it blew up with a tremendous explosion and broke in half. It sank in about five minutes. It was identified as a freighter of Africa Maru class, 9500 tons gross.

It is evident from these reports that the sub commanders of WWII were a very special breed indeed. They would plan and track the enemy for hours, only to have to change tactics radically at the last second. Yet they still managed to put a torpedo or two into the target to put it on the bottom. These brave men and their crews are true American heroes and they have not received the credit which is due them and which they have earned. They played a major role in shortening the war in the Pacific by cutting Japan's supply lines and reducing their ability to defend their island empire.

Glossary

Glossary

aft
Near or toward the back of a boat.

amidships
Near or toward the middle of a boat.

angle-on-the-bow
The angle from the target track to the line of sight as seen from the target bow.

beam
The widest part of a ship. Also, to the side of a ship.

bearing
The direction in which you are looking, either through your binoculars or the scope.

bow
The forward part of a ship.

bridge
The position from which the captain commands the vessel during all surface attacks.

COMSUBPAC
Commander of submarines Pacific Fleet.

conning tower
The position from which the captain commands the sub on all submerged attack actions.

DD
Designation for a destroyer.

DE
Designation for a destroyer escort.

dive bubble
Indicator used to measure the angle of a dive.

dive planes
Large metal winglike structures located fore and aft used to force the bow up to surface, or down to dive.

exec
Executive Officer, or XO. Second-in-command aboard a sub.

fathom
A unit of measuring depth equal to six feet.

flank speed
The full speed of a ship.

gyro
A gyroscopic device inside U.S. torpedoes which enabled them to be set to travel on a specified angle, or course, after leaving the sub.

heading
The direction of a ship's travel measured in degrees from 0 to 359.

helm
The position in the control room from which the vessel is steered.

keel
The main support of a ship which extends its entire length. Frequently used to describe a ship's bottom.

knot
Unit of speed on ships. It's equal to one nautical mile (6080.27 feet) per hour.

line of sight
An imaginary line from your position to another object.

magnetic detonator
A device used in some U.S. torpedoes which would cause the torpedo to explode if it passed under the keel of a ship. It knows when to blow itself up by measuring changes in magnetic fields.

mark
A term used during target tracking which means: Take an instrument reading now.

maru
Japanese term for merchant ship.

pointing the target
Constantly changing your heading to present the minimum profile to the enemy.

port
The left side of a ship when facing forward.

range
The distance to the target.

rudder
A plane mounted vertically on a ship's stern used to change the ship's heading, or direction.

SJ
Surface radar.

sonar
A method of locating and measuring the range of objects in water by sending out a sound signal, listening for a reflection of that signal of an object (ship or sub), and measuring the time interval between sending the signal and receiving the reflected signal. Also, sometimes used to mean listening passively for sounds with a hydrophone, a device for picking up sounds underwater.

starboard
The right side of a ship when facing forward.

stern
The rear of a ship.

TBT
Target Bearing Transmitter. This device consisted of a pair of binoculars, mounted on the bridge of a sub, which would transmit the direction it was pointed. This information was sent below to the Torpedo Data Computer.

TDC
Torpedo Data Computer. This was a mechanical, analog computing device used in subs to solve the target-tracking equation when given a set of input data. The data consisted of the target range, heading, and speed. Once a firing solution was determined, the TDC would automatically transmit the proper gyro setting to the torpedoes.

test depth
The maximum known safe depth which a submarine hull can withstand. Going deeper than this was possible, but dangerous.

thermocline
Also temperature gradient or temperature layer. This is the dividing line between layers of water of different temperatures. Once below this layer, a submarine is difficult to find with sonar because the layer is reflective.

track
A line referring to a course, or line of travel.

trim
Refers to the process of moving water in and out of the tanks aboard a sub to stabilize the boat at a given depth.

torpedo volume
The number of torpedoes fired at a target.

Ultra
Refers to secret radio messages giving sub commanders the location of enemy convoys. This information was usually obtained by breaking Japanese radio codes.

wolf-pack
The practice of having more than one sub work together to attack enemy shipping.

Suggested Reading List

If you would like more information on submarine tactics or life aboard a submarine, I would recommend the following books:

Bagnasco, Erminio. 1973. *Submarines of World War II*. Naval Institute Press.

Beach, Edward L. 1972. *Dust on the Sea*. Holt Rhinehart.

Beach, Edward L. 1955. *Run Silent, Run Deep*. Holt Rhinehart.

Compton-Hall, Commander Richard. 1982. *The Underwater War 1939–1945*. Blandford Press.

Cremer, Peter. 1984. *U-Boat Commander*. Naval Institute Press.

Holt, Edwin P. 1983. *Bowfin*. Avon.

Lockwood, Admiral Charles A. 1951. *Sink 'em All: Submarine Warfare in the Pacific*. E.P. Dutton.

O'kane, Admiral Richard. 1981. *Clear the Bridge!* Bantam War Books.

Stern, Robert. 1983. *U.S. Subs in Action*. Squadron/Signal Publications.

Theodore, Roscoe. 1949. *United States Submarine Operations of World War II*. Naval Institute Press.

Index